T0103316

# ANOTHER GOSPEL

# ANOTHER GOSPEL

*Christian Nationalism and*
*the Crisis of Evangelical Identity*

Joel Looper

WILLIAM B. EERDMANS PUBLISHING COMPANY
GRAND RAPIDS, MICHIGAN

Wm. B. Eerdmans Publishing Co.
4035 Park East Court SE, Grand Rapids, Michigan 49546
www.eerdmans.com

© 2024 Joel Looper
All rights reserved
Published 2024
Printed in the United States of America

30  29  28  27  26  25  24      1  2  3  4  5  6  7

ISBN 978-0-8028-8427-5

**Library of Congress Cataloging-in-Publication Data**

A catalog record for this book is available from the Library
of Congress.

# CONTENTS

.

# PREFACE

This book was conceived as a coauthored project with my father, Shayne Looper, columnist and then pastor of Lockwood Community Church in Coldwater, Michigan. Though adding this project on top of his other commitments while preparing for retirement proved impossible, his imprint remains on the pages below. To be sure, he does not agree with everything I have written here. (Read his column on related subjects to get a sense of his position.) Further, had he been part of this project, we would have taken a quite different tack on the book's subject. The polemical tone that shows up in many passages would be far less prominent if not absent; personal examples where the Christian-nationalist gospel has affected congregations would have sat alongside points from church history; and we would have added practical steps congregations could take to address the false gospel of Christian nationalism. The biblical theology undergirding the whole would, I think, have remained basically the same.

The volume I actually wrote, which you hold in your hands, is significantly shorter than the one we envisioned, and, though it was written in only a few months, it developed through years of conversations with Justin Lee, associate editor at *First Things*. Not a few readers will have had conversations similar to those Lee and I had during the Trump era: ones about the culture war, the future of the church in general and evangelicalism in particular, and the way the church should relate to national politics. Like so many others, our discussions sometimes get too heated; we find ourselves stuck on the same mutually exasperating points. Unlike so many others, however, these conversations have been productive. As much as anything, this book is an attempt to sum up the position at which I have arrived, and the one Lee, as I understand it, has (with significant caveats) rejected. Not that I expect Lee and his theological compatriots to immediately change their minds and accede that my diagnosis of what ails the American church was actually right all along. But I do expect that at least some who find themselves bogged down in debates like ours—and even those more acrimonious than ours—will find that this slim volume provides a way forward.

I intend this book to be provocative. That will be immediately obvious, and I am keenly aware of the dangers and drawbacks such an approach presents today. My hope is that the argument that much of American evangelicalism has placed its faith in a different, nationalist gospel may provide a clear, theologically grounded place to begin discussions about Christian nationalism, Trump support, and the culture war. Perhaps others who see further than I will be able to apply this argument in ways that help the evangelical movement see itself as *church* again. If in these difficult years evangelicals came to the conclusion that any serious conversation about

Christian theology and politics must invariably begin with the nature and mission of the church as *gospel-formed community*, the movement would have made an invaluable advance.

All quotes from the Scriptures refer to the New International Version (NIV) unless otherwise indicated. Though numerous people have contributed to this book through editorial advice, conversation, and debate, any errors in fact or judgment in the pages that follow are mine alone.

Thanks to Arc.digital, a worthy and unique webzine where parts of chapter 4 originally appeared as "Putin's Christian Nationalism." Thanks to Hope Fellowship, a community who has been with us through thick and thin. Thanks to Barry Harvey and our longstanding Monday reading group at Southern Roots in Waco, Texas, a group where my theology of the church began to take its present form. Thanks also to Barry for convincing me that "Another Gospel" is the right title. Thanks to my parents, Justin Lee, Mark Nation, and Joe and Nancy Gatlin, and numerous others who read and commented on the whole book or particular chapters. Thanks especially to Anali Gatlin Looper, who undertook a much-needed edit of the first chapters while recovering from surgery and has loved me even in trying times. Finally, I'm grateful to God for Daniela Bea, whose inquisitiveness, spunk, and beautiful smile continue to bring so much life and joy to our house. This book is dedicated to you.

# 1

## A GOSPEL PEOPLE?

"Hey, sir, I'm here with Eric Metaxas."

Pennsylvania State Senator Douglas Mastriano looked serious, perhaps even a little nervous. Wearing a baseball cap that read "Desert Storm Veteran" and ensconced in a simple home office, Mastriano had the caller on speakerphone, which served to bring the audience in on the conversation. "He wants to know if you want any message to go out on his show today."

The date was November 30, 2020; the forum, Eric Metaxas's immensely popular Christian podcast, *The Eric Metaxas Show*.[1] The subject—and what other subject of conversation was there for Americans in November 2020?—was Donald Trump's claim that the presidential election had been stolen from him through massive voter fraud, "ballot dumps," and other conspiratorial activities engineered by the Democratic Party and other bad actors.

Then a familiar voice came loud and clear through Mastriano's phone. "Eric is fantastic, by the way."

"Can you hear him, Eric?"

"Yes, I can hear the president," Metaxas says, visibly agitated. "Mr. President, I want to know, what can I do?"

"Fantastic," Trump says. "Your whole show and your whole deal is great, so just keep it up. We're making a lot of progress, actually."

"We will not abandon this fight," Metaxas says. "This is the most horrible thing that's ever happened in the history of our nation, and I just want to know, what can I tell my audience?"

In response, Trump takes the audience back to the November 3 presidential election when early in the night, before mail-in ballots were counted in Pennsylvania, Georgia, and certain other states, it appeared he might win. In the days that followed, a period lengthened considerably because of the COVID-19 pandemic and the volume of mail-in ballots, Joe Biden passed Trump's tally, eventually building a lead of about seven million votes and seventy-four electoral college votes. That dramatic reversal of fortunes, the president tells Metaxas's audience, was "the greatest scam in the history of our country."

"We are going to win," Metaxas says in response. "Jesus is with us in this fight for liberty. There was a prayer call last night, and you cannot believe the prayers that are going up. This is God's battle even more than it is our battle."

"Let me tell you, so I'm going to give you a little example. The Supreme Court ruling you had the other day on churches, you're allowed to go to church, actually," Trump says, referencing state and local restrictions on churches put in place to stop the spread of COVID-19. "That was all because of me. That was my three people [whom he nominated as justices] who voted."

However, Trump warns, "if we don't win this thing, we'll never be able to bring our country back."

"I would be happy to die in this fight," Metaxas says. "This is a fight for everything. God is with us."

Metaxas was and is far from alone among evangelicals and other conservative Christians in believing Trump's claims about the 2020 election. Twelve days after this podcast episode aired, the first Jericho March participants converged on Washington, DC. Marchers prayed that God would intervene and dramatically reinstate Trump—the last buffer, many feared, between them and religious persecution. Advertisements for the nominally interfaith event read "Let the church ROAR!" Shofars were blown, internationally recognized speakers inspired the crowd, and leaders prayed in tongues and prophesied. The conspiracy theorists Alex Jones, Mike Lindell and Michael Flynn, as well as Archbishop Carlo Viganò, Dinesh D'Souza, and Metaxas spoke, some referencing God and religious freedom in the same breath as the QAnon conspiracy theory that Democratic leaders and other elites are involved in a massive pedophile ring. All of these men connected right worship of God and reverence for country, and all thought Christians must "stop the steal" and reinstate the forty-fifth president.

The organizers then scheduled another rally for January 4 and 5, the days before the US Senate would certify the results of the 2020 election. Participants at that rally prayed that Vice President Mike Pence would intervene and stop the certification of the election, a power which certain right-wing commentators inaccurately claimed the vice president held. Reenacting Judges 6, participants blew shofars and marched seven times around the Supreme Court, then seven times around the Capitol building, the idea being that, like the walls of Jericho, the corrupt edifice of Democratic power that had stolen the election and the country would come tumbling down.

Neither institution's walls crumbled that day, but, as everyone knows, the next day many of those praying for God's intervention tried to intervene to stop Biden's win themselves. After a pro-Trump rally in which Christian music blared over loudspeakers and a cross and a gallows were set up on the lawn, thousands, perhaps as many as ten thousand people, stormed police barricades, broke windows in the Capitol building, beat police officers (in one case with an American flag), destroyed property, and searched the premises for Vice President Mike Pence, House Minority Leader Nancy Pelosi, and other lawmakers. Signs that read "Jesus saves," "Make America godly again," and "God, guns, and guts made America"; a Christian flag; Bibles; and other religious paraphernalia were seen in the midst of the mob. Some in the crowd shouted, "Hang Mike Pence." Others sped through the hallways yelling "Naaaaaaancy" in what can only be described as a murderous tone. Still others chased a Black Capitol police officer through the building as he risked his life to lead them away from lawmakers. One insurrectionist, Ashli Babbitt, was shot to death inside the Capitol when she tried to climb through a police barricade. One hundred thirty-eight police officers were injured, fifteen badly enough to require hospitalization.

While all this was going on, Jacob Chansley, the so-called QAnon Shaman, and a large group gathered in the Senate chambers. Mounting the dais where Mike Pence had been presiding over the certification of the election minutes before, he stopped fellow insurrectionists from riffling through the senators' papers and personal effects long enough to offer up a prayer.

> Thank you, Heavenly Father, for gracing us with this opportunity to stand up for our God-given inalienable rights. Thank you, Heavenly Father, for being the inspiration needed to these police officers to allow us into the building, to allow us to exercise our rights, to allow us to send a message to all the tyrants, the communists, and the globalists, that this is our nation, not theirs, that we will not allow the America, the American way of the United States of America, to go down. Thank you, divine, omniscient, omnipotent, and omnipresent creator God, for filling this chamber with your white light and love, with your white light of harmony. Thank you for filling this chamber with patriots that love you. And that love Christ. Thank you, divine, omniscient, omnipotent, and omnipresent creator God, for blessing each and every one of us here and now. Thank you, divine creator God, for surrounding and filling us with the divine omnipresent white light of love and protection, peace and harmony. Thank you for allowing the United States of America to be reborn. Thank you for allowing us to get rid of the communists, the globalists, and the traitors within our government. We love you and we thank you in Christ's holy name, amen!

Chansley's New Age-tinged theology didn't stop him from offering a prayer that his evangelical compatriots could wholeheartedly affirm. The whole crowd roared amen like you yell "break" coming out of a football huddle—or, perhaps, how in the movies medieval knights with swords unsheathed and the cross emblazoned on their shields rush into battle. For all the world, it appeared to be what *The Atlantic*'s Emma Green called it: a "Christian insurrection."[2]

Dig into what that phrase means—no, merely ask a random churchgoing American what the word *Christian* means—and a gulf opens up between those who will tell you the protest-gone-wrong at the Capitol could be an expression of vibrant, committed Christian faith and those who see what happened that day as a symptom of apostasy. Each side assumes the other has sold their souls to party politics. Each counts the contemptuous ways they "tell the truth" about their opponents on Facebook and Twitter as high art. Those opponents, by contrast, foment violence with agitprop and lies that any "honest" person will condemn. Few ask what happened to the fruit of the Spirit among us. Fewer still ask if their political opponents could spot that fruit in their lives.

Everyone knows the American church has a problem. Hardly anyone thinks they're part of it.

Many of the men and women at the rally on January 6 and some who broke into the Capitol identify as evangelical Christians. For this and other reasons, evangelical identity has been at the heart of the scandals that today have shaken the American church to its foundations. I too have called myself evangelical. Those who first discipled me taught that evangelicalism stood first and foremost for fidelity to the gospel, and I believed them. In fact, that claim is in the very name of the movement. The word *evangelical* comes from *euangelion*, the Greek word used in the New Testament for gospel, the good news about Jesus Christ. Evangelicals may disagree about how best to articulate that good news, some emphasizing the incarnation, others the cross or the resurrection, and still others the Spirit's abiding power. But all would agree, at least theoretically, that what God did through Jesus of Nazareth is the hinge upon which the history of the world turned.

For all of their problems, evangelicals identify themselves as people who live by the light of what Jesus did, people for whom the gospel is everything.

After January 6, however, a question came to mind that I haven't been able to shake: *Which* gospel do evangelicals believe is *everything*? Because according to Scripture, getting ensnared in a false gospel is both spiritually deadly and entirely possible.

Less than two decades after the crucifixion, the apostle Paul accused a controversy-plagued group of churches in what is now south-central Turkey of this very thing:

> I am astonished that you are so quickly deserting the one who called you in the grace of Christ and are turning to a different gospel—not that there is another gospel, but there are some who are confusing you and want to pervert the gospel of Christ. But even if we or an angel from heaven should proclaim to you a gospel contrary to what we proclaimed to you, let that one be accursed! As we have said before, so now I repeat, if anyone proclaims to you a gospel contrary to what you received, let that one be accursed! (Gal. 1:6–9)

The "different gospel" Paul meant was one in which gentile converts to Christianity had to get circumcised, follow the whole Jewish law including the food laws, and, in short, become Jewish. This gospel said that you had to become a part of the Jewish nation to be a Christian. Paul responded, perhaps immoderately, that he wished the circumcising faction would just go the whole way and "cut it off" (Gal. 4:12). He was hot under the collar. Why? Because it was through faith in what Christ had done that the Galatians could be saved and *not* through Jewish culture. The true gospel, Paul writes, had even been announced to Abraham in the breathtaking promise "All nations will be blessed through you" (Gal. 3:8; Gen. 12:3).

"Listen!" Paul wrote. "I, Paul, am telling you that if you let yourselves be circumcised, Christ will be of no benefit to you. Once again I testify to every man who lets himself be circumcised that he is obligated to obey the entire law. You who want to be justified by the law have cut yourselves off from Christ; you have fallen away from grace" (Gal. 5:2-4 NRSV).

In Acts 15, a pivotal chapter in Saint Luke's theological history of the early church, this controversy reached Jerusalem. Paul and his ministry partner Barnabas had tangled in the city of Antioch with educated, pious Jewish Christians who taught that "unless you are circumcised according to the custom taught by Moses, you cannot be saved" (15:1). Finally, Peter, James, and the other apostles themselves got involved, and the elders of the Jerusalem church met to work through this fraught question.

There came a point in this discussion, however, when Peter couldn't take it anymore. He became emotional, pointing out that the gentiles too had received the Holy Spirit and the gift of faith, and he didn't blanch at drawing some dramatic conclusions from this fact. "He did not discriminate between us and them, for he purified their hearts by faith. Now then, why do you try to test God by putting on the necks of Gentiles a yoke that neither we nor our ancestors have been able to bear? No! We believe it is through the grace of our Lord Jesus that we are saved, just as they are" (Acts 15:9–11).

For those who have spent a lot of time in church, all this might just seem like good Christian talk. "Grace, grace, God's grace," we sing, then the pastor says the same thing for twenty or forty minutes and we're on our way home to catch opening kickoff. It might seem, dare we say, obvious.

But read Peter's speech again, carefully this time. What he says isn't what you might expect. He didn't say, "The gentiles are saved by the grace of the Lord Jesus, just as we are," so we should let them "come as they are." He says precisely the opposite, that *Jews like him* require the gift of grace just like the gentiles. Everyone at that emotionally charged church meeting in Jerusalem agreed that you don't need to be an *ethnic* Jew to be a Christian. That wasn't even up for debate. What they bitterly disagreed about was the role of Jewish culture and the heritage of Israel in the newly formed Jesus movement. The question was whether the nation of Israel or the new universal church embodied what God had in store for humanity.

This should hardly surprise us. God, not an ancient, perhaps mythical lawgiver, had given the Jews their law in the Old Testament. Through rabbinical teaching, centuries of temple sacrifice, stories passed down the generations, national festivals, and much more, that God-given law became the mold in which their nation's culture was shaped. Naturally then, telling gentile converts to the *Jewish* Messiah that they didn't need to keep the law must have seemed worse than absurd to some of Paul and Peter's Jewish opponents. It must have seemed blasphemous, a way of rejecting everything God had done in the history of their nation while still claiming Christ with one's lips. If there really was only one Lord, one faith, and one baptism (Eph. 4:5) as Paul and some others taught, that put gentiles on a level with Jews in a way that seemed to devalue Israel. These men and women had grown up and lived their lives knowing that their people were exceptional. *They* were chosen by Yahweh. *They* were children of Abraham. And now some in their own movement, often the people most certain that Jesus was the Jewish Messiah, were abandoning their nation at the very moment God was redeeming Israel. This, they doubtless said to one another, is a fight for all that is good and holy. As Eric Metaxas put it two thousand years later, "This is a fight for everything."

Nevertheless, Paul would call their gospel "another gospel"—that is, not gospel at all. Let them be cursed, he said, literally "anathema." Then he repeats himself just so the Galatians are sure they read him right. Why use such vitriolic language? Because the Jewish culture warriors whom we call "Judaizers" had identified themselves with and organized their lives around a community other than the one universal church, the community that is supposed to be shaped in its life together by its allegiance to Jesus. In other words, they were basing their lives on a story that was not the Christian story. Instead, these men identified themselves first and foremost with the nation of Israel, its culture, and its future.

The Judaizers must have thought this was the only reasonable place to lodge their hopes, not with these revisionists who would disregard the commands of God at the very moment the Christ has come and the kingdom is dawning.

They trusted in the marks of being a good Jew: circumcision, meticulous attention to Sabbath and food laws, and a passionate, unrelenting nationalism. And they believed that Christ, the Messiah, had come to redeem *their* people, that *they* were the locus of God's work in the world.

But Paul called this trying to be saved by "the works of the law" and opposed it to faith in what Jesus had done. There's a misunderstanding we should avoid here. When Paul said "works of the law," he didn't mean trying to earn your salvation through good deeds or by measuring up to some abstract moral law. What abstract moral law is summed up by talking about circumcision? No, when Paul used the phrase "works of the law," he meant works of the *Jewish* law, the pride and joy of *the nation* his theological opponents loved so much. He meant that being a good Jew was not the aim of Christian faith. And he fully understood what sort of reaction this might elicit from other Jews. If you disregarded these boundary markers or implied that God's favor sometimes rested on gentiles rather than Jews (as Jesus himself did in Luke 4:16-30), you might literally get murdered.

That didn't stop Paul for a moment. The difference between what they believed and the gospel he had been tasked to proclaim was that important.

See what large letters I make when I am writing in my own hand! It is those who want to make a good showing in the flesh that try to compel you to be circumcised— only that they may not be persecuted for the cross of Christ. Even the circumcised do not themselves obey the law, but they want you to be circumcised so that that they may boast about your flesh. May I never boast of any-

thing except the cross of our Lord Jesus Christ, by which
the world has been crucified to me, and I to the world. For
neither circumcision nor uncircumcision is anything; but
a new creation is everything! (Gal. 6:11–15 NRSV)

The heartfelt beliefs of Paul's opponents in Galatia and
those Peter debated in Acts 15 were about the goodness and
uprightness of *Israel* and therefore *themselves* rather than the
goodness and justice of *God*. This is why they were anathe-
matized. But this brings up the question that has haunted me
since January 6, 2021. Is that true of American evangelicalism
too? Have we as a movement really committed ourselves to
the goodness and justice of God? Or is our real allegiance to
our subculture's vision of what America should be? Do we as a
movement even really understand the difference?

It has been increasingly difficult for me to deny hearing
an echo of the Judaizers' "other gospel" among American
evangelicals today, and I attribute this to what has been called
Christian nationalism. Christian nationalism might be defined in any number of ways. Some might mention people
who want prayer and Bible reading back in schools and the
Ten Commandments on the courthouse steps. Others point
out those who call America a Christian nation and claim
that the nation is in danger of falling away if the Democrats
gain power but will remain in God's good graces if we pull
the lever for the Republicans. But in every case, Christian
nationalists see it as their job to take America back for God
and for "real" Americans—the community with which they
identify themselves.

As with the Judaizers before them, Christian nationalists
appear to trade the community of the one universal church

and its life for the community of the nation, sanctifying and blessing a particular cultural and political vision of America. This explains why for some people the performance of Christian religiosity and Christian cultural trappings become boundary markers in judging who is or is not a real American. It also helps us grasp the otherwise preposterous view that a certain limited-government reading of the American Constitution can serve as evidence that you're a follower of Jesus of Nazareth.

This displacement of the church has other odd effects. Immigration by *other Christians* from Central America fleeing poverty and violence is thought by Christian nationalists to be a threat to Christianity in the United States. National laws about abortion, the LGBTQ movement, and even voting rights seem like an existential threat to the individual Christian's ability to obey his or her Lord; not Christ, but the government, as Trump put it, says that you can go to church. Donald Trump must be a Christian or a "baby Christian" because he is on "our" side—that is, he supports our cultural and political vision of America. I could go on.

Like the Galatians two millennia ago, I fear that evangelicals have forgotten the way the church is supposed to live in the world because we have exchanged the gospel about Jesus for "another gospel." Just look around you: the fruits of the Spirit are deemed irrelevant to the real Christian business of owning the "libs." God and the Bible can be "hurt," as President Trump said in August 2020, because both function primarily as parts of "our" way of life.[3] God as such is not the God who judges us and offers a qualitatively different kind of life, but the God who justifies the way we already live. We live in fear or at least a perpetual state of anxiety about how national politics will affect us. Deception, slander, hatred, impiety, sexual immorality, cowardice, greed, and practical unbelief are excused because, we tell ourselves, what our political opponents are doing is so much worse.

"But are they *not* worse?" you might ask. "Why criticize conservatives and not liberals—unless you're just another Big Evangelical making nice with the world to line your pocketbook?"

Since suspicion and open malice have become the norm among believers when it comes to politics, and few think to be ashamed of this state of affairs, I should lay my cards on the table. No, my purpose in writing this book is not to recruit you for the Democratic Party. My positions on gay marriage, the trans movement, and abortion all align with traditional evangelical theology. Though many churches refuse to lift a finger to lighten the burdens of our celibate gay and lesbian brothers and sisters and thus leave the law of Christ unfulfilled, I nevertheless believe those churches are right to ask celibacy of them. I have no qualms about calling abortion abhorrent and the trans movement an utterly confused ideology leaving multitudes of wounded in its wake.

In another book, I have taken aim at liberal Constantinianism or, to redeploy Gustavo Gutiérrez's term, the progressive hope of building a "profane Christendom."[4] Such Americanized theology, which often verged into open heresy, has for the last century been the bigger problem in mainline denominations, and even today as many liberal clergy hail the end of Christendom, they continue to use their pulpits to denounce government actions and laws they see as contrary to the "spirit of Jesus." The fact is that America has always had significant numbers of *liberal* Christian nationalists, and they will occasionally come in for criticism below. They are not my tribe, and I have no truck with their theology.

Why focus my attention on conservatives then? The answer should be obvious: most of us evangelicals are conservative. "Examine yourselves!" Paul exhorted those he discipled, and we cannot do that while obsessing about what others are doing. Ask yourself: *what has our gospel wrought among us?* Has it made us more like Jesus? If the truthful answer is "not really," perhaps the reason is that we've got the wrong gospel.

Of course, none of this is new. The marriage of Trumpism, "stop the steal," and Christian culture—or, better, Christian nationalism and evangelicalism—is not a Vegas wedding after which the partners just go back to their lives (and their other families) on Monday morning. It had been in the works for a very long time. If this were untrue, the Public Religion Research Institution (PRRI) would have found more than 8 percent of evangelicals interested in considering why conservative Christians had been instrumental in the insurrection.[5] Among evangelicals, 57 percent would not have blamed antifa. And many evangelical leaders would not have reacted to the events at the Capitol as if their religious faith had been put at risk (which, if their faith is Christian nationalism, it had).

> There is no doubt the election was fraudulent. That is the same today as yesterday. There is no doubt Antifa infiltrated the protesters today and planned this. This is

political theater and anyone who buys it is a sucker. Fight
for justice and Pray for justice. God bless America!

—Eric Metaxas (@ericmetaxas),

January 7, 2021[6]

There's a reason one of the most secure buildings on the
planet had an easy breach on one of the most important
and guarded days in history. They were allowed. The
paid rioters have changed the game. It's a smokescreen
to frame true Patriots.

—Pastor Greg Locke (@pastorlocke),

January 6, 2021[7]

This seems consistent with several of the Trumpsters
who insist the people who broke the windows were not
#MAGA at all.

—Dinesh D'Souza (@DineshDSouza),

January 6, 2021[8]

An unarmed mother was shot and killed by police in the
Capitol today. Why isn't "say her name" trending? Why
aren't any of the people who rioted over "police brutality" speaking out? Is it because you're all utterly full of
sh*t?

—Matt Walsh (@MattWalshBlog),

January 7, 2021[9]

Question: Was today's protest "mostly peaceful," like all
the ones last summer were?

—Dr. Darrell Scott (@PastorDScott),

January 7, 2021[10]

Each of these tweets has a subtext. Good conservative Christians, the white hats, real red-blooded Americans—or, in words doubtless spoken around dinner tables around middle America on January 6, 2021, "our people"—would never despise the rule of law, assault police officers, and involve themselves in what the rest of the world witnessed that day. If they did, agent provocateurs sent by the other side must have tricked them into it. *Because our people are the good guys.*

These evangelical pundits came to these conclusions because trusting their eyes and ears meant risking "everything"—that is, their hopes for the future and the faith communities with which they identified themselves. In other words, January 6 jeopardized the very gospel of conservative America.

Think about it. Say, for the sake of argument, that the men who wrote the above tweets were right in every detail about what happened that day, that the insurrection was a massive conspiracy to defame Donald Trump and the American right. That would dispel precisely none of the concerns I have raised about these evangelical influencers' allegiance to Christ. Would their tweets lead *anyone* to believe the church was the primary community with which they identified and that the story about Jesus is the fundamental fact that orders their day-to-day lives? Or do these men, whether they realize it or not, subscribe to "another gospel" about the goodness of a conservative, patriotic, distinctly American way of life and a "church" of "real Americans" like them? As the theologian Karl Barth said of Christians, "their politics can only be a form of their actual life."[11] Their politics reflect a certain view of the nation, not the church's proclamation, and that makes it crystal clear what they think life is really about. We must call this other gospel what it is: anathema.

Those who embrace this anti-gospel are cursed because just as no one will be justified before God by observing the Jewish law (Gal. 3:11), no one will be justified before God by living as a "real" American or a good citizen. To put your hope in the gospel of America means that you are cut off from grace. If the outcome of an election means "everything" to you, the new creation cannot mean anything.

By the time the first generation of Christians died, many churches around the Mediterranean world likely found Paul's heated rhetoric in his letter to the Galatians and the emotion of the Jerusalem council less and less relevant. That is because Jews had gone from making up the entire church to being a miniscule percentage of a rapidly growing international movement. The notion that you had to take on Jewish cultural mores to be a Christian had gone the way of all the earth. Instead, by the end of the first century, conflict arose between the almost entirely gentile church and non-Christian Jews about who could rightly lay claim to the Bible.

Maybe it was the terrible war with Rome that by AD 70 had leveled Jerusalem and the temple. Maybe it was a host of other historical and sociological factors. But the question that occasioned some of Paul's most famous writings got turned around. It now seemed to many that if you were a Jew, you *shouldn't* or even *couldn't* be a Christian. While there is much we cannot know at this historical distance, we can be certain of one thing: for many Jews, joining the church had come to look like a betrayal of their nation. And most chose their nation.

American Christians today appear poised to make the

same choice. Since the late 1960s many liberal Protestants have slipped into a brand of Americanized Christianity without realizing it. The worship of God gradually came to seem extraneous to their primary task of community activism, nonprofit work, and getting out the vote, and the Democratic Party slowly displaced the church as their primary community. As the nation secularized and the gulf between the demands of the culture and the demands of the church widened, more and more liberal Christians have woken up one morning to realize that, while their core allegiances remained the same, they have no clear reason left to continue calling themselves Christians. Sunday morning has been reduced to a gathering of like-minded do-gooders hoping for connection and inspiration. Brunch and a mimosa met more of their felt needs.

Evangelicals are on their way to a similar fate. The Republican Party, the flag and the armed forces, family values and rough-and-tumble individualism can, it turns out, all be had more easily without Jesus. From 2018 to 2019, the Southern Baptist Convention lost more than 2 percent of its total membership, and during the pandemic that rate seems only to have increased.[12] Some might counter that quite a few Americans adopted evangelicalism during the Trump years. And that is true. But nowadays becoming "evangelical" no longer needs to involve regular church attendance, and saying the sinner's prayer or having a personal relationship with Jesus is strictly optional. Instead, the word has morphed into a synonym for Republican or cultural conservative. Today one in five Muslims in the United States and a significant percentage of Hindus identify as evangelical.[13] Then there are the masses of people, particularly in the South, who call themselves evangelical yet never go to church.[14] Committed inerrantists regarding biblical authority and staunch opponents of gay marriage, they find it too burdensome to practice evangelical sexual ethics or maintain openness to those in need. The data is clear. Given enough time, most of us in the evangelical movement—or, at any rate, our children—will just be traditionalist, individualist, conservative, and passionately patriotic Americans. But not Christians.

What can be done to stop this long slide? Not much that is within human power. God himself will have to change us, reorient us toward the gospel in our communal and political lives. We wait for the coming of that powerful, revivifying word. Our part in that day will be what it has always been: hearing and obeying.

But we can put ourselves in a better position to hear that word. We can, to use the biblical language, "prepare the way," clearing away barriers and issues in our individual and collective lives that make it harder to hear when God speaks to us. Why, we should ask ourselves, is it so natural for us to tell God-stories *apart from* the larger story of what Christ is doing in the world through the church? Why, despite all the Bible says to the contrary, do we continue to speak of faith as an individual matter that is "just between me and Jesus"? When did the nation and national politics become so much a part of how we think of ourselves *as Christians* and the church so trivial for our faith?

Addressing these questions is among the most critical tasks for the American church today. Doing so will open us to the future God has for the church by helping us better understand our past collective sin, how we as the American church have missed the mark. Seeking these answers is, in other words, an act of repentance, which in the Greek literally means "change your mind" (*metanoia*). If we dare open ourselves to repentance and ask whether allegiance to Christ demands a change of mind, we must understand how we as American evangelicals came to this difficult place in our history. It is, therefore, to church history that we must turn.

# 2

# BAPTIZING
# THE NATIONAL BODY

There has never been a time that the church lived out the gospel perfectly. Even in New Testament-era Christian communities—the "early church" many hold up as a near-perfect model of gospel living—we find men in relationships with their stepmothers, indifference and disrespect toward the poor, deceit about money, damaging heresies, and, yes, instances of cultural and political loyalties taking precedence over the body of Christ. The apostles dealt with all these issues and more, and this side of Christ's return we can hardly expect to be spared similar difficulties.

So we should ditch our idealized pictures of the early church. Great, you say. Easily done. But seeing more clearly what the Bible says about the church's first years hardly means we should throw the baby out with the bathwater and label every age of the church as equally holy or execrable. Christians living in some times and places have understood what the church is and why we gather on Sunday mornings (or whenever) better than others. Take, for example, the Epistle to Diognetus, one of the earliest Christian writings outside the New Testament, a letter written not to Christians but to an interested outsider. The anonymous author explains the fledgling Christian movement like this:

> For Christians are not distinguished from the rest of humanity by country, language, or custom. For nowhere do they live in cities of their own, nor do they speak some unusual dialect, nor do they practice an eccentric lifestyle. This teaching of theirs has not been discovered by the thought and reflection of ingenious men, nor do they promote any human doctrine, as some do. But while they live in both Greek and barbarian cities, as each one's lot was cast, and follow the local customs in dress and food and other aspects of life, at the same time they demonstrate the remarkable and admittedly unusual character of their own citizenship. They live in their own countries, but only as aliens [*paroikoi*]; they participate in everything as citizens, and endure everything as foreigners. Every foreign country is their fatherland, and every fatherland is foreign.[1]

This description would have been as astonishing and offensive to well-bred ancient ears as it is to many in our day. You can imagine what Diognetus's response to his Christian friend must have been: *So Christians participate in the life of their country, whether Rome or elsewhere—but you're telling me that their hearts aren't completely in it and they might conceivably forsake their civic duties and jump ship if their God tells them to do so? Don't they appreciate Roman freedoms and the greatness of the empire? Forgive me, but it sounds like in certain situations you Christians might be likely to commit treason.*

If Diognetus had such a thought, he would have been right. By contrast, American Christians, whether they call the United States a "Christian nation" or not, usually just assume we should feel at home here. Something must be deeply wrong, we think, if society or governments make it hard to live the Christian life.

But the first Christians disagreed, and they had biblical warrant for approaching life this way. "Dear friends," we read in 1 Peter 2:11, "I urge you, as foreigners [*paroikous*] and exiles, to abstain from sinful desires, which wage war against your soul." The first readers of this letter weren't just *spiritual* foreigners and exiles. Both Peter and the Epistle to Diognetus describe Christians as people who live outside the power structures of their societies. That's because their allegiance was not to Caesar, their community wasn't the empire, and the orientation of their lives wasn't directed toward securing a future for themselves or their children. Their citizenship was "remarkable and admittedly unusual" because, as Paul put it in Philippians 3:20, that citizenship was "in heaven." Here on earth, the author of the Epistle to Diognetus writes, they prepare themselves to lose out and be dealt with unfairly, to "endure everything as foreigners." Because that's what they are.

Such a view of what Christians could expect in this world sometimes brought out astonishing courage and self-giving among church leaders, and leaders expected the same from their people. In the first years of the second century, Ignatius, who was bishop of Antioch in Syria, was arrested and carted away to Rome to be thrown to the lions in the Coliseum. As he got nearer to the Eternal City and the fate he knew awaited him there, he wrote letters to a number of churches, including the one in Ephesus, and his message to them still has the power to astonish and trouble us.

> Pray continually for the rest of mankind as well, that they may find God, for there is in them hope for repentance. Therefore allow them to be instructed by you, at least by your deeds. In response to their anger, be gentle; in response to their boasts, be humble; in response to their slander, offer prayers; in response to their errors, be "steadfast in the faith"; in response to their cruelty, be gentle; do not be eager to retaliate against them. Let us show ourselves their brothers by our forbearance, and let us be eager to be imitators of the Lord, to see who can be the more wronged, who the more cheated, who the more rejected, in order that no weed of the devil might be found among you, but that with complete purity and self-control you may abide in Christ Jesus physically and spiritually.[2]

These are the words of a man being persecuted by the state for his Christian faith, a man we have every reason to believe was literally ripped apart by wild animals for other people's entertainment not long after writing this letter. Yet Ignatius wanted his fellow believers to show themselves to be "brothers" to their persecutors by—what, by just *taking it*? Apparently so.

But why, we want to ask this ancient bishop, should his congregation of persecuted Christians just take it? Why not fight for the rights of other Christians, or at least Christians who were Roman citizens? That might well earn the church more say in the wider society in the long run. Then Christians would be able to do more good and make society more just. Why should Ignatius encourage his people to acquiesce to horrific injustice when they are the ones being persecuted? Does not the very gospel he preached say that they too, not just those yet to be saved, are infinitely valuable to God? Does the Bible not teach that God hates injustice?

Don't just take it from the powers that be, some would tell Ignatius's people. Take the empire for God.

I have come to see that this position is only answered effectively by telling a story. In a few pages we will explain why American Christianity, despite the religious freedom that was born here, fell into many of the same traps as earlier Christendom. But first we need to describe how, two hundred years after Ignatius sent this uncanny exhortation to the community of Christians in Ephesus, the empire was indeed taken for God. Unimaginable as it was to Ignatius and his generation, the Edict of Milan issued by emperor Constantine in AD 313 legalized Christianity and began favoring the church through financial support and other means.

Christians, or the vast majority of them at any rate, were overjoyed by Constantine's rise and the stunning, seemingly providential developments that came with it. Eusebius of Caesarea wrote the first book-length church history during these years, and he ended the book with the astonishing triumph of the first Christian emperor:

> His adversary thus finally thrown down, the mighty victor Constantine, pre-eminent in every virtue that true religion can confer, with his son Crispus, an emperor most dear to God and in every way resembling his father, won back their own eastern lands and reunited the

Roman Empire into a single whole, bringing it all under their peaceful sway, in a wide circle embracing north and south alike from the east to the farthest west. Men had now lost all fear of their former oppressors; day after day they kept dazzling festival; light was everywhere, and men who once dared not look up greeted each other with smiling faces and shining eyes. They danced and sang in city and country alike, giving honour first of all to God our Sovereign Lord, as they had been instructed, and then to the pious emperor with his sons, so dear to God. Old troubles were forgotten, and all irreligion passed into oblivion; good things present were enjoyed, those yet to come eagerly awaited. In every city the victorious emperor published decrees full of humanity and laws that gave proof of munificence and true piety. Thus tyranny had been purged away, and the kingdom that was theirs was preserved securely and without question for Constantine and his sons alone. They, having made it their first task to wipe the world clean from hatred of God, rejoiced in the blessings that He had conferred upon them, and, by the things they did for all men to see, displayed love of virtue and love of God, devotion and thankfulness to the Almighty.[3]

By AD 390 the Roman world and the way that society perceived the faith had changed completely. Christianity had become the religion of the state. When the emperor Theodosius ordered or allowed a massacre of civilians in Thessalonica by Roman troops, Saint Ambrose, the bishop of Milan, ordered the emperor to repent and denied him the Eucharist until he did so. Though the events that followed are themselves shrouded in myth, the emperor is said to have knelt before the powerful churchman and begged for absolution. It must have seemed to many as if the kingdom of God had finally, fully arrived.

A year later, Theodosius outlawed the worship of other gods. Being a Christian and being a good citizen of the empire had looked more and more alike in the three generations since Constantine's reign. Now after an awkward period that witnessed the rise of monasticism and imperial intervention in Christian theological disputes, people began to think they were one and the same thing. It became impossible to get anywhere in Roman society without being a Christian.

Echoes of the older way of thinking about the Christian life were still common. Saint Augustine says in the first lines of his *City of God* that that city "dwells by faith as a pilgrim among the ungodly" awaiting "the final victory" while the earthly city "seeks mastery" and "is itself mastered by the lust for mastery even though all the nations serve it."[4] Augustine used the language of pilgrimage frequently. He knew that Christians should not feel too at home in the world. He also knew that "in this world, the two cities are indeed entangled and mingled with one another."[5] The tares could not be uprooted before the last judgment without harming the wheat.

Yet Augustine's vision of a good church-state settlement also made the tares much harder to see. He praised Theodosius because he "did not cease from the very beginning of his principate to assist the Church in her labours against the ungodly by means of the most just and merciful laws."[6] In fact, Augustine gushed, "He commanded that the statues of the heathen should be everywhere overthrown, well knowing that not even earthly rewards are placed in the power of demons, but in that of the true God." Being a good Christian and being a good Roman had become, for all intents and purposes, indistinguishable. The empire had indeed been taken for God. And, as many Christians had promised, in some ways the state did become more just. But there was a problem. Despite Augustine's talk of Christians being pilgrims and foreigners, most of the rank-and-file faithful had made themselves very much at home in the late empire. They didn't resist desire as Peter urged them. The "lust for mastery the nations serve" that Augustine had warned about had infiltrated the church itself, passed itself off as pious zeal or concern for justice and right worship and, unbeknownst to many, began to rule in the name of the gospel.

More than a millennium elapsed between this time and the Protestant Reformation. God didn't, contrary to what many evangelicals have been taught, get fed up and leave the medieval church to its own devices. Quite the contrary. The gospel still went forth. Believers grew and discipled others inside and outside the monasteries and great cathedral towns. Great works of art, theology, philosophy, and architecture appeared, blessing the church and humanity. The so-called dark ages were anything but.

Yet the notion that before the return of Christ the world should or could be run by the church maintained a tight grip on the Christian imagination. "Two there are by which this world is ruled," Pope Gelasius I wrote to the emperor in the eastern capital of Byzantium, bringing to expression the relationship between spiritual and civil authority most people in the late fifth century already took for granted.[7] Since the papacy had control over increasingly extensive territories in central Italy, it became more and more necessary for them to have armies at their disposal. And the popes used them. They provided security, to be sure. But they also launched crusades—and, frequently enough, papal land grabs. Several times men seized the chair of Saint Peter by violence, and on more than one occasion rival popes backed by different political factions vied for power. Pope Julius II, who held the reins in Rome until the eve of the Reformation and earned the nickname "the warrior pope" through his leadership of military campaigns against other Italian powers, chose his pontifical name because he wanted to be like Julius Caesar.

When the Reformation did happen, it shook the foundations of the European social order.

Yet most churches that came out of the Reformation—that includes, for example, Lutherans, the Reformed, and Anglicans—changed little of the Catholic church-state arrangement. In fact, they made matters worse by identifying the church still more firmly with the new, more centralized form of the nation-state that was emerging in Europe at that time. To be sure, Martin Luther had sometimes affirmed that the church, not governments, should deal with heresy, and the civil authority did indeed deal less often with theological matters.[8] Nevertheless, John Calvin's Geneva, Ulrich Zwingli's Zurich, and many other Protestant cities executed heretics in the decades after Luther nailed his "Ninety-Five Theses" to the Wittenberg Castle Church's door. This fact alone shows how intertwined Protestantism had become with the self-understanding and stability of these cities and nations. Being a good Protestant was a necessary part of being a good Zuricher or Genoese or Englishman.

During the early Middle Ages there had been, at least theoretically, one universal church. After the Reformation, it became increasingly clear that European believers identified more with their prince or ethnic group than the body of Christ, a community for which by definition national borders can mean nothing. Far from being foreigners and living like citizens of another, heavenly city, Western Christians fought, tortured, and killed other Christians under the sign of the cross on behalf of their princes and nation-states. The body of Christ has continued to be fractured by national conflict down to the present day.

Now then, you might be thinking, can we put that dreary part of church history behind us? Let's get on to the birth of religious freedom; the biblical conviction and courage of radical, free church Protestants; and the separation of church and state in America.

That is indeed the plan. But the road and the destination will not be as (usually) advertised. The Christian communities Diognetus heard about from his Christian correspondent did not reappear in the modern West after 1776. In fact, we'll find that, in certain ways, the situation of the church actually got worse, not better, with the advent of American Christianity.

This story begins not with the Reformation, but in Britain. The Radical Reformation—a catch-all term for Anabaptists, Spiritualists, and other radical Protestants who found no support from the powers that be—never found a firm hold on the continent outside of a few isolated communities. Things unfolded quite differently in England, however, and there we find the roots of nearly all non-mainline Protestant denominations in America today, including Baptists, Congregationalists, Methodists, Quakers, and more. These Anglo-Saxon theological innovators were very different from the German and Dutch-speaking Anabaptist communities that took root on the continent. They took critical steps away from how Christianity had been practiced to date and critical steps toward modern open societies and democracy. And when it came to religious radicalism, the Puritan elite who led the expeditions that established Jamestown and Plymouth colonies in America were of this ilk. Often enough, their radical preaching went hand and glove with extreme individualism and an intense nationalism.

Think, for example, of John Milton, the author of the poem *Paradise Lost* and, at the time anyway, a notorious political radical. An advocate of freedom of religion, freedom of conscience, and freedom of the press; an apologist for king-killers; and a purveyor of ideas similar to those the American revolutionaries would lay hold of a century later, Milton's religion sometimes looks almost evangelical.

> God in much displeasure gave a king to the *Israelites*, and imputed it a sin to them that they sought one: but Christ apparently forbids his disciples to admit of any such heathenish government: *the kings of the gentiles,* saith he, *exercise lordship over them; and they that exercise authority upon them, are called benefactors. But ye shall not be so: but he that is greatest among you, let him be as the younger; and he that is chief, as he that serveth.* . . . That he speaks of civil government, is manifest by the former part of the comparison, which infers the other part to be always in the same kind. And what government comes nearer to this precept of Christ, than a free Commonwealth; wherein they who are greatest, are perpetual servants

and drudges to the public at their own cost and charges, neglect their own affairs; yet are not elevated above their brethren, live soberly in their families, walk the streets as other men, may be spoken to freely, familiarly, friendly, without adoration.[9]

For those put off by Milton's old-style language, here's a quick summary: Christ told his disciples not to lord it over each other like gentile rulers do. Instead, he taught us that if anyone wants to be great in the kingdom of God, he or she has to be the servant of all. In this gospel passage found in Matthew 20:25 and Luke 22:25, Milton argues that Christ clearly means that Christians should live in a free country without kings lording it over us, and our rulers should be normal, regular, accessible people who work very hard for the public good.

What, you ask, is my hang-up here? Not Milton's preferred form of government. Personally, I think there is a lot to like in freedom of the press, freedom of religion, democratic elections, and the rest. The issue here is with Milton's exegesis and its unintended consequences. Jesus's first disciples were a small band of illiterate fishermen in a backwater province of the Roman Empire. They had never heard of a "free commonwealth" and could have had no idea that those who followed them would one day lead nations. Even if for some reason Jesus had wanted to offer them instructions on democratic governance, they had no context for it. So, contrary to Milton's argument, Jesus's point here cannot be about national politics. The community Christ means, the people he exhorts to live politically in a completely different way, is clearly the community of his followers, what would soon be called the church. Milton's slippery exegesis may sound nice to our American ears, but it has nasty consequences: it erases the church and replaces it with the nation.

The radical Protestants of Milton's generation who came to America for religious freedom were little different from the famous poet on this score. Ever heard the language of "city on a hill" from Matthew 5:14 applied to America? Many American presidents have used it this way, and, as a matter of fact, that use of the phrase comes from the Puritan John Winthrop, the founder of the Massachusetts Bay colony. In a 1609 lecture given on the ship before he and his companions embarked on the treacherous sea journey from England to the New World, Winthrop told those assembled that the whole world would be watching them. Their virtue and their way of life would be an example for everyone. To make this point, he poached Jesus's metaphor, which originally applied to the church, and used it to exalt his new American community.

Like Winthrop, when politicians today speak of America as a city on a hill, what they're doing, whether they realize it or not, is having the United States take on the church's role in the world. *America* is the beacon of hope for humanity. *America* is God's plan for the world. *America*—and, by implication, not the church—is the new Israel. To be sure, this heresy (because that is what it is) has hardly been uncommon in countries with majority Christian populations. You can see it in medieval England or early modern Switzerland, modern Germany or Argentina, and, as we will see later, today one finds it in rare form in Vladimir Putin's Russia, where belief in the holiness of the nation has been the primary motivation for war. The form of this "other gospel" that arose in the United

States, however, is unique and potentially worse than those found in other countries.

This might sound like America-bashing. It's not. I mean that instead of the church being enlisted in accomplishing whatever the state thinks best (as happened in other countries), in America right from the get-go the church was absorbed into the nation. The British Catholic G. K. Chesterton once said that America has the soul of a church, but Ralph Wood and Stanley Hauerwas were more clear-eyed when they wrote that the church in America has the soul of the nation.[10] And this happened for historical reasons we all learned in school but few stop to think about.

So let's think again about these early Americans, especially those hardy people with political and religious beliefs like Milton's who left England during and immediately following the English Civil War to avoid persecution. The dissenters that later became Congregationalists settled in New England, the Quakers clustered in Pennsylvania, Catholics tended to end up in Maryland, and over the next century countless other groups from England, Germany, the low countries and elsewhere carved out a spot for themselves in the countryside. Ever since, people have thought of America as a safe haven for refugees of political and religious persecution. As Will Herberg, author of *Protestant, Catholic, Jew*, wrote more than two generations ago, "The newcomer is expected to change many things about him as he becomes American—nationality, language, culture. One thing, however, he is *not* expected to change—and that is his religion."[11]

But what happened when these peoples from different countries and ethnic groups with incompatible theological commitments came together to form a society and a government? Their sheer diversity threatened anarchy. And if one religious group came to hold most of the power in Washington, persecution of religious minorities could happen just like it had in Europe. But, on the other hand, asking massive numbers of people to change religions was completely impossible. Just the fact of being in a new land was already destabilizing for people, and even more than today people in past centuries felt that their religion was a fundamental part of their personal and communal identities.

What to do? How could individuals within all this astonishing diversity attain a stable identity, a place where they individually and collectively felt at home? "American reality not only raised the question," Herberg wrote, "it also supplied the answer."[12]

That answer was the First Amendment to the Constitution, a guarantee that their right of religious freedom would be protected: "Congress shall make no law respecting an establishment of religion, or prohibiting the free exercise thereof." Or, rather, the First Amendment was half the answer. Because, as great as the First Amendment was and is, it did nothing by itself to bind Americans together. The danger that theological, biblical, or religious disagreements would divide the new country remained very real.

The second part of the answer was that freedom of religion was guaranteed not just by law, but by the nation. That is, Americans' shared commitment and love for our system of government and the American way of life is really what preserves religious freedom, not just what Congress or the Supreme Court says. Without that collective commitment, the laws and even the Constitution itself wouldn't be worth the paper they're written on and churches wouldn't be guaranteed the freedom of worship. This led American Christians to make a fatal assumption: that the bond to one another as Americans comes before and makes possible our bonds to other Christians within the church.

It came to seem natural—Christian, even—that Americans would set aside certain biblical and theological commitments they held in order to take part in American society. Quakers knew they might have to set aside pacifism to participate fully in national politics. Lutherans may need to shelve certain theological commitments they had about government. Catholics would sometimes be expected to set aside the dictates of Rome in favor of those hashed out in Washington, DC. American Christianity gradually boiled down to a set of broad, culturally shared ethical commitments. To be sure, this allowed the United States to develop a grand national story and identity that changed the world forever, but American Christians purchased this shared identity and this national story by trading in our identity in the one, holy, catholic, and apostolic church.

Now that, you might be thinking, is a provocative claim. Indeed. But the displacement of the church in American Christianity and its replacement with the nation is clearly traceable in American history. The effects of this displacement can, of course, be rather mundane. But at other times they have been deeply disquieting.

Remember the Amalekites from the Old Testament? They attacked Israel at the most vulnerable point in its history: after the Exodus while they were wandering in the wilderness. Prophecies then came that God would have them return the favor once they had secured possession of the promised land, and the name of Amalek, chief of the Amalekites, became a byword in Israel.

In fact, it still is. Since Hamas's vile October 7, 2023, terrorist attack on Israelis, Prime Minister Benjamin Netanyahu has used the word to justify the slaughter of Palestinians.[13]

So then, if America took the place of the church and thinks of itself as the new Israel, we might expect other players in American life to be assigned biblical roles too. You have probably already guessed who the Amalekites were: native Americans.

In the very speech Winthrop spoke about his group of Americans-to-be as a city on a hill, he warned them not to disobey God like King Saul had by failing to destroy Amalek. Whatever Winthrop meant by that, Americans after him compared the native peoples they knew to the ancient tribes who attacked God's people—and used it as biblical sanction for genocide. The historian of American religion John Corrigan found this language being used (and criticized) as recently as the mid-nineteenth century.[14] That's exactly the same period the idea of manifest destiny got regular Americans believing that God really did want their nation to rule the entire continent. And that might mean getting some blood on your boots. The massacres that "opened the west," many apparently thought, jived just fine with serious Christian commitment.[15]

Native peoples were hardly the only ones relegated to the ever-shrinking area outside the American city on a hill where there was weeping and gnashing of teeth. Sometimes other *Christians* found themselves refused entry to the church of America. When the political and cultural tumult that led to the American revolution ramped up in the early 1760s, Americans had seen themselves as the new Israel for more than a century. In these years, naturally enough, England became ancient Egypt in the eyes of many. Over and over, American writers cried out that they were being made slaves because the British crown had imposed (really pretty light) taxes on them while not giving them representation in parliament. Many of these very American men had themselves purchased actual enslaved people of African descent, but it occurred to few that they'd be more appropriately cast as Pharaoh than as the Hebrews. Their budding national story didn't allow them to be cast in that role.

Of course, slavery, like the centuries-long genocide carried out against native Americans, *was* condemned by some believers, and not just on the grounds that it violated the spirit of the American founding documents. This was a time in American history when people knew the Bible, and they quoted it frequently in arguments about public policy. For a few, the thought sank in that the universal church, not the American project, was the continuation of the biblical story, and that realization affected their politics. But for most, even those who had eyes to see the world-historical evil that was American slavery, the Bible was only a treasured part of their American heritage. They hardly sensed that they were part of a divinely authored community that included people of every tongue, tribe, and nation.

Abraham Lincoln too had this blind spot. The sixteenth president sometimes attended but never joined a church. He believed in God and freely spoke of "Providence" but had little use for church doctrine, and in his youth even the barebones, modern type of religion we find in his mature political speeches left him uncomfortable. On the other hand, his trust in and love for the spirit of 1776 and the political principles the country inherited from that generation might well be dubbed religious. One sees this in the Gettysburg Address, the most famous lines Lincoln ever spoke:

We have come to dedicate a portion of that field, as a final resting place for those who here gave their lives that that nation might live. It is altogether fitting and proper that we should do this.

But, in a larger sense, we can not dedicate—we can not consecrate—we can not hallow—this ground. The brave men, living and dead, who struggled here, have consecrated it, far above our poor power to add or detract. The world will little note, nor long remember what we say here, but it can never forget what they did here. It is for us the living, rather, to be dedicated here to the unfinished work which they who fought here have thus far so nobly advanced. It is rather for us to be here dedicated to the great task remaining before us—that from these honored dead we take increased devotion to that cause for which they gave the last full measure of devotion—that we here highly resolve that these dead shall not have died in vain—that this nation, under God, shall have a new birth of freedom—and that government of the people, by the people, for the people, shall not perish from the earth.

Many Americans memorize this speech in school, and nearly all of us find ourselves moved by its noble beauty. Yet even here, if we read carefully, we find that the Christian story of God's work through the church has been artfully dislodged from its scriptural context and reset inside the American story. Lincoln's rhetorical move is beautiful—and perilous for the true faith. The soldiers buried on the battlefield made the ultimate sacrifice to redeem their country. They have become little Christs through whose shed blood the "nation might live." Even this early in our nation's history, the military has become America's savior and redeemer, and this could only happen because the nation had first assumed the place of the church as the primary vehicle for God's work in the world. And Lincoln has hardly been unique in making this move. Every modern American president makes it too.

Only one speech in post-revolutionary US history gets more airplay than Lincoln's, and only one American can less safely be criticized in polite company. I mean Martin Luther King Jr. and his "I Have a Dream" speech. There are good and obvious reasons to withhold criticism from Dr. King, particularly today. I could have picked plenty of other examples. But he remains America's most important public theologian, and his work has irrevocably shaped American culture and the American church. In particular, this speech, given on August 28, 1963, at the Lincoln Memorial before a crowd of 250,000 people, is among the most powerful pieces of oratory in modern history. It looms large in our collective unconscious, and, God willing, it always will.

But that does not mean it is holy writ. King was in his time subject to the same intellectual and culture forces that affected others of his generation. His professors and dissertation adviser at Boston University had been educated when the twentieth century was being called "the Christian century," and many then felt that the world and American society were finally coming under the sway of Christian thinking. Jesus was often called an "ideal." He provided a roadmap for a good and just society. That meant industry and government were in the crosshairs of most every pastor and parachurch organization in the land, and, especially early in the century, intense optimism was in the air that they would achieve their aim. King was onboard for their entire project. Until the very end of his life, he too believed that America could be Christianized.

These theological assumptions about America—the very ones so many American Christians before him have held—are on full display in the "I Have a Dream" speech. Take a moment and look again at the end of the speech.

> So even though we face the difficulties of today and tomorrow, I still have a dream. It is a dream deeply rooted in the American dream. I have a dream that one day this nation will rise up and live out the true meaning of its creed: We hold these truths to be self-evident, that all men are created equal. . . .
>
> I have a dream that one day every valley shall be exalted, every hill and mountain shall be made low, the rough places will be made plain, and the crooked places will be made straight, and the glory of the Lord shall be revealed, and all flesh shall see it together. . . .
>
> This will be the day when all of God's children will be able to sing with new meaning: My country, 'tis of thee, sweet land of liberty, of thee I sing. Land where my fathers died, land of the pilgrims' pride, from every mountainside, let freedom ring. . . .

We resonate so deeply with King's vision because here, many feel, we experience like nowhere else the power of Christ's message in our time. Here we have a hope and a faith that joins "all God's children" in a "symphony of brotherhood," one that empowered King and those with him to "work together, to pray together, to struggle together, to go to jail together, to stand up for freedom together, knowing that we will be free one day." Here we have an eschatology straight out of Isaiah 40 applied to us, a vision of the day of the Lord that King described earlier in the speech by quoting Amos: "justice rolls down like waters and righteousness like a mighty stream." Here we have what in our time has become a rare and precious thing: the pure Christian gospel preached in power for all to hear.

Or do we? Seen through the lens of 1 Peter and the Letter to Diognetus, even here that vision and that gospel is cut short. Because in King's dream, it is not the one, holy, catholic, and apostolic church that proclaims to all the people of the earth that Christ's life, death, and resurrection has changed everything. It is not the body of Christ that embodies and lives out the kingdom in the here and now, showing all and sundry what communion with Christ will look like when it comes in its fullness. Instead, it is *the American people* and all like-minded people around the world—what is sometimes referred to as the "beloved community"—who proclaim a gospel about America and democracy, progress and freedom. That gospel is drawn at least partially from the scripture of the Declaration of Independence and the Constitution. Far from being pilgrims and foreigners on this earth who have set their hopes on another country, the children of God in King's dream aim to make America great, if not again, for the first time. Even here, at the peak of what the American religious tradition has to offer, "another gospel" has surreptitiously begun to insert itself.

In his last years, King's understanding of his prophetic calling widened. He felt compelled even against the advice of his staff and supporters to speak out against the Vietnam

War. Upon learning that more American whites lived in poverty than Blacks, he began to advocate for the complete restructuring of the American economy. With the US military presence in South Asia still polling well and the memory of the Cuban Missile Crisis fresh, these were not positions likely to draw grant money or, for that matter, the support of moderate whites. By 1967 the demands of the Poor People's Campaign, dissatisfaction among radicals with his commitment to nonviolence, and the toll taken by years on the road under the constant threat of assassination were beginning to weigh on King. He believed less and less that any of the whites in power could be depended upon. He was increasingly depressed. His star was fading and with it his influence. Yet he felt the responsibility for getting results, for achieving real justice, was on his shoulders.

The night before his assassination, King preached at a church in Memphis, Tennessee. The sanctuary was sweltering, and, when he first mounted the platform, he seemed on edge. Yet as sometimes happened, the Baptist pastor warmed to his theme. After some dark months, King seemed almost like his old self.

> Well, I don't know what will happen now. We've got some difficult days ahead. But it really doesn't matter with me now, because I've been to the mountaintop. And I don't mind. Like anybody, I would like to live a long life. Longevity has its place. But I'm not concerned about that now. I just want to do God's will. And He's allowed me to go up to the mountain. And I've looked over. And I've seen the Promised Land. I may not get there with you. But I want you to know tonight, that we, as a people, will

get to the Promised Land. So I'm happy, tonight. I'm not worried about anything. I'm not fearing any man! Mine eyes have seen the glory of the coming of the Lord!

There is something natural and even right about King putting himself in the place of Moses. In Deuteronomy 34 Moses was allowed to look from Mount Nebo into the promised land. But he would not be allowed to join his people there. King, feeling the threat of death, knew very well that he might be in the same position. There is also something natural and right about putting African Americans in the place of Israel. They too came out of slavery. They too hoped for centuries in the Lord's redemption and still suffered under the weight of injustice in the years that followed.

But something more, something fundamental has to be added to qualify the "naturalness" of King's rhetorical move here. Otherwise, we risk losing the thread of the gospel story. The addition we mean is this: The identity of Black American Christians cannot primarily be that they're Black or that they're American. Their participation in the body of Christ, the one universal church, makes that impossible. Being a Christian is an identity that, when push comes to shove, forces all other identities to the periphery. It radically relativizes all other claims to our allegiance, no matter how compelling they might seem.

Something deeply worthwhile can be gained through metaphorically identifying Black America (or even the "Beloved Community," whatever that is) with Israel. Yet biblically speaking, the church—and there is only one church!—is to be identified with Israel, and no one else. Like Israel, the church's promised land cannot be gained through human strength,

45

goodness, or ingenuity. It's not a relative justice, a social or political settlement in which everyone finally has enough. It's not something *we* can achieve at all. No, the church does not just work for the common good, for justice, or for as many people as possible to identify as Christians. The church *witnesses*. We point forward into the future, toward what, on the basis of Christ's life, death, and resurrection, we expect him to do to set the world right. All other such hopes, including those noble hopes King himself held, will sooner or later be dashed. History is a slaughter bench. As we should all know by now, its arc does not of its own accord bend toward justice. As long as Christ tarries, the world is never going to stop being the world. And America and its founding vision are very much a part of the world.

All these men—Winthrop, Lincoln, and King—knew the Bible inside and out. They all claimed Christ as Lord and, in different degrees, the orthodox Christian faith. None realized that the belief that America has been chosen by God cannot coexist with the faith once given. Unless, that is, the faith is in the process of being subtly subverted by "another gospel," the gospel of America, which is no gospel at all.

We can reliably sketch the doctrine of the religion which preaches this American gospel. Fifty years ago the sociologist Robert Bellah wrote that "there actually exists alongside of and rather clearly differentiated from the churches an elaborate and well-institutionalized civil religion in America."[16] The God of America is envisioned as "rather 'unitarian'" and "on the austere side, much more related to order, law and right than to salvation and love. Even though he is somewhat deist in cast, he is by no means simply a watchmaker God. He is actively interested and involved in history, with a special concern for America."[17] A light to the nations and a city on a hill, America is where God is moving today, and it is the object of his special favor. The eschatological hope of this religion is that the whole world would finally believe in America, live as we live, and adopt our civil religion or, as we often say, our "values."[18] Finally, servicemen and women have "shed their blood for us" so that we might be free—which perhaps explains why every president from Washington down to the present has mentioned God in his inaugural address, but not one has mentioned Jesus Christ.

Christianity is not and never has been the American civil religion. Bellah is correct about that. Or, to say the same thing a different way, the United States is not a Christian nation and never was. But what Bellah missed is something that concerns us far more than how the United States gets labeled. He missed that the American civil religion—"another gospel," perhaps the most beguiling one on offer today—is being practiced *within* our churches.

Above all, in evangelical churches.

# 3

# THE SCANDAL OF
# THE EVANGELICAL HEART

When the *Los Angeles Times* interviewed Billy Graham about his old friend and golfing buddy Richard Nixon in 1990, the man many thought of as America's pastor said that he still found the Watergate controversy mystifying and thought most Americans did too.[1] "The only thing that bothered me about the whole thing was the [explicit] language that [Nixon] used on the tapes," Graham said of the damning Oval Office recordings that led to Nixon's resignation, later adding, "I didn't believe it was the real Nixon. And, of course, I believe in supernatural powers, of both good and evil, and I think some of these were at work at the time."

Yes, Graham had listened to the relevant recordings, presumably including the tape on which Nixon seems to instruct Bob Haldeman to cover up the break-in at the Democratic National Committee headquarters at the Watergate building. "We're up against an enemy, a conspiracy," Nixon said at one point. "They're using any means. We are going to use any means. Is that clear? I don't give a sh-t about the law. I really need a son of a b---- who will work his butt off and do it dishonorably." Such moments were hardly rare for Nixon. But Graham felt for whatever reason that the media had magnified Nixon's shortcomings. Initially America's pastor seemed more shocked by Nixon's foul mouth than by what the president was communicating in tapes like this one. Future generations, Graham was quite sure, would view these matters very differently since they could look back on Watergate without the progressive media constantly whispering in their ear.

Graham never seems to have understood—or, better, never wanted to understand—the paranoid, self-righteous, conniving, and power-hungry man to whom he had yoked himself. And even after he recognized something was wrong or at least dangerous about marrying the pulpit and national politics, he continued to make unforced errors in his relationships with politicians. As Graham biographer Grant Wacker put it, he "fell off the wagon several times. The lure was too great entirely to resist."[2]

Here America's pastor stands in sharp contrast to much of our generation's evangelical leadership. Today's conservative Christian Trump supporters aren't falling off the wagon. They're on the bandwagon. They have known or, at any rate, should have known from the very beginning who Donald Trump is. Unlike Nixon, his tapes were public before his supporters ever went to the polls, no one batted an eye at his foul language, and a breaking and entering charge would have sounded bush-league compared to the accusations Trump faced. Nevertheless, even at his lowest moments he had their full-throated support anyway.

Everyone knows the reason why. Almost without exception, those who voted for Trump did so to save America from liberals. Their laments about the country's direction usually hit a few familiar notes: "Communists" and "cultural Marxists" dominate the Democratic Party. They aim to undermine the American free enterprise system and make Judeo-Christian morality a thing of the past. They want public schools to teach that children can choose their gender and how and with whom to express their sexuality. LGBTQ people, Blacks, and immigrants are favored while white, heterosexual boys are second-class citizens. The morality of commitment to family is being actively undermined. These leftists' goal, stated or otherwise, is to drive Christians out of public life and make standing up for Christian principles in the workplace impossible. And, most Trump voters will add at this point in their apocalyptic litany of warnings, it is already happening. The American life we have known hangs by a thread. Only the willfully blind, brainwashed, or dishonest—this is a particularly common accusation—refuse to admit that these evil people are coming for us.

Almost everyone has been on the receiving end of a speech like this, whether the orator was your neighbor, Tucker Carlson, or a late-night host satirizing conservative politics. Today, often enough, evangelicals are themselves the orators and audience for such harangues. That alone shows just how much has changed since Billy Graham's heyday.

A recent article in *First Things* describes how many evangelicals view that change.[3] American society's relationship to Christianity, Aaron Renn argued, has undergone a massive shift in a fairly short period of time. He called the period before 1994 the "positive world," in which society as a whole was positively disposed toward Christianity.[4] Then came the "neutral world" period, which lasted until 2014, the year *Obergefell* legalized same-sex marriage nationally. Since then, he says, American Christians have lived in a "negative world," a situation in which society as a whole takes a negative, even hostile view of Christianity—and this necessitates new strategies, new missional approaches, and new ways of thinking among Christians.

As Renn sees it, Rod Dreher's book *The Benedict Option* presented almost the only negative-world approach on offer. In that book, Dreher, an Eastern Orthodox writer and former blogger for the *American Conservative*, takes readers through the life disciplines of communities that live by the Rule of Saint Benedict, the most famous monastic rule in the Western church. The rule is ancient, produced in the sixth century, and it has been in use ever since. Practicing such a rule of life inculcates spiritual disciplines that American culture today finds absurd or even threatening. To maintain such ways of life in the face of stiff resistance, you need community, patience, and time. In the book's final pages, Dreher defines the Benedict option as "a call to undertaking the long and patient work of reclaiming the real world from the artifice, alienation, and atomization of modern life."[5]

Dreher is rightly concerned about the disorder surrounding the life of the mind and sex in today's culture, a disorder that many see as synonymous with freedom or at least inseparable from it. The situation is so bad, he suggests, that the only move Christians have left is a (partial) withdrawal from mass society, and he lays out some strategies to help Christians manage that withdrawal. The goal is to preserve whatever cultural and spiritual goods we can through the "dark age" Dreher suggests is even now coming upon Western society.

*The Benedict Option* appears to offer the church a way forward in a post-Constantinian age, an age where Christianity is no longer a major factor in shaping culture and society in the West. But appearances can be deceiving. Read carefully, and you will find that Dreher's strategy of withdrawal is a *backup plan*. The observant reader will see this part of Dreher's theology come into her peripheral vision several times in *The Benedict Option*, but none more clearly than when he addresses religious freedom:

> Though orthodox Christians have to embrace localism because they can no longer expect to influence Washington politics as they once could, there is one cause that should receive all the attention they have left for national politics: religious liberty.
>
> Religious liberty is critically important to the Benedict Option. Without a robust and successful defense of First Amendment protections, Christians will not be able to build the communal institutions that are vital to maintaining our identity and values. What's more, Christians who don't act decisively within the embattled zone of freedom we have now are wasting precious time—time that may run out faster than we think.[6]

Dreher's parallel *polis* or, as he later puts it, a robust counterculture only becomes necessary for evangelicals and other conservative Christians "because they can no longer expect to influence Washington politics as they once could." If the situation were otherwise and the West still thought of itself as Christendom, he would have no reason to see withdrawal as the task of the hour. Even now though, Dreher assumes religious liberty must act as a tool to gain and hold as much

ground for the church as possible. To be sure, Dreher emphasizes that religious liberty "is not an end in itself" and that
the church's goal is "not political success but fidelity."[7] He
does see, at least in part, what the church is called to be. Yet
his prescription in *The Benedict Option* (to say nothing of his
other work) leads Christians not to adopt a posture of service
and self-sacrifice toward the world, but to fight those outside
the church tooth and nail for political territory, even if that
fight is seen as primarily defensive rather than offensive.[8]

There is, I should add, one negative-world strategy evangelicals have adopted that Renn neglected to mention: the
Trump strategy. That he overlooked it is more than a little
odd. It is far and away the most popular negative-world strategy among evangelicals today, and the one Renn himself
seems to endorse. You can vote for DeSantis, or Haley, or,
theoretically, a Democrat and still be a Trump-strategy man
or woman. You may never have pulled the lever for Trump at
all. The Trump strategy claims that, when it comes to faith in
public life, the church and world are two teams, and in this
winner-take-all game, the best defense is a good offense. It
is, if one looks with clear eyes, just Constantinianism for a
negative world.

Put another way, the Trump strategy is the Moral Majority strategy retooled for a minority-Christian America.
Jerry Falwell Sr., founder of the Moral Majority, would tell
students at Liberty University that "your mission is to save
America, and from the base of American freedom, to evan-
gelize the world."[9] Falwell called America a Christian nation.
He expected that many Americans were outraged by the
1962 *Engel v. Vitale* ruling that prohibited school-sponsored
prayer. Above all, he believed that the church's proclamation

and public policy should ideally work hand in glove, and he fought to see this hope realized.

The Trump-strategy adherent fights for exactly the same thing but sees the political landscape before him differently. America is secularizing. Christians are losing influence in government, major institutions, and in the media. Their opposition to same-sex marriage and the transgender movement have made traditionally minded evangelicals very powerful enemies. Obviously then, the fight will be harder. One will be less likely to win through kind, winsome means—or, as the oft-used phrase goes, "with one hand tied behind your back." Like Nixon, the Trump strategist feels that he must use any means to take back American for God—and, of course, for himself and his children.

All Trump strategists countenance such baptized Machiavellianism, and all think working for the kingdom means marrying Christianity and public policy to some degree. Pew Research found that 45 percent of Americans want America to be a Christian nation, and though far fewer meant that non-Christians should be second-class citizens or that the church should be the author of public policy, serious theocrats do find allies among the rest of that 45 percent.[10] Winning may mean different things to different Trump strategists, but for all of them, winning the culture war defines their political outlook and, for the most part, their faith.

Pastor Robert Jeffress, an early and fervent Trump devotee, summed it up by saying, "I want the meanest, toughest SOB I can find to protect this nation. And so that's why Trump's tone doesn't bother me."[11] When Jeffress and other Trump strategists talk about protecting the nation, they mean something more than the time-honored bipartisan rite of flooding the military with money. They want protection for the national culture they see as traditionally American. They want Christian institutions to be able to enshrine their beliefs in organizational policy without getting sued or losing tax-exempt status. They want, in short, to retain some of the positive and neutral worlds *within* the negative world by forcing the rest of the country to do right by them. The only way to do that is political action through the federal government. And in a negative world—one in which Christians come ever closer to being a minority, and committed evangelicals and conservative Catholics become a rarity in our culture-making institutions—those ends require downright Machiavellian means.

The rest of this book could easily be spent working through views like Dreher's, Renn's, and Jeffress's, then going issue by issue in an attempt to sift truth from fantasy. I might dive into the Christian Reconstructionist movement among the Reformed theological progeny of Rousas Rushdoony or the increasing influence of the charismatic and Pentecostal New Apostolic Reformation, both of which subscribe to theocratic Dominionist theology.[12] Or I could lay out in excruciating detail everything the new Catholic integralist crowd gets wrong. I might plead with the Trump-strategy-sympathetic evangelical reader (who, again, may never have actually voted for the forty-fifth president) to see that their cure for what ails America is worse than the disease. I could rehash every immoral, foolish, and despicable word and deed of Trump's campaign and presidency.

I won't. All that has been done time and again. Instead, for the sake of argument, I will simply *assume* the Trump-strategy-sympathetic evangelical can succeed. Say the cultural and political situation is every bit as bad as they think and worse. Say that persecution of Christians is already here or right around the corner. Say electing Trump or another culture warrior really is our only chance to save America from liberal tyranny.

Even then there is a prior issue few evangelicals have seriously considered, one that dwarfs the fate of the American republic in importance: *how the Trump strategy affects the life and witness of the church.* The reader knows my answer already: it encourages Christians to identify the nation rather than the church as their primary community and to practice America's politics rather than the politics of Jesus. It encourages us to believe *another gospel*, the gospel of America, which is no gospel at all.

Some readers will want numbers, graphs, and sociological studies to bear out this claim or as many case studies as we can get our hands on. But neither will help us quantify this scandal of the evangelical heart. The better path, I think, is to pick a maximalist Trump strategist to be our dialogue partner. The goal for him has to be total Christian dominance in both political and cultural spheres, for the mechanisms of government to encourage the spread and acceptance of the gospel. This writer wants "so much winning" for conservative Christians that even lite-variety Christian nationalists "get bored with winning." Against the background of his work, it will be easier to tell whether our argument that evangelical Trump strategists have abandoned the gospel is right. If indeed the shoe fits, other evangelicals and conservative Christians will be left to ask themselves whether and to what degree it fits them too.

The interlocutor I have in mind is Stephen Wolfe, an institutionally independent political scientist, proud right-wing Presbyterian, and author of *The Case for Christian Nationalism*. Wolfe wants the United States to identify itself as a Christian nation, impose laws that preference conservative Protestant Christians and their ways of life, and discriminate against those whose actions or ways of life might interfere with that moral and political order. But just as clearly he wants to reaffirm the nation's Western cultural heritage, which includes an ethnic heritage. In fact, in Wolfe's mind Protestantism and our Western ethnic-cultural traditions are of a piece. Like the church and public policy for Falwell and the Moral Majority, Wolfe sees Protestantism working hand in glove with traditional Western culture, and this, he argues, will make America the best and most just society it can be. It's these commitments that lead Wolfe to call himself a Christian nationalist: "The Gospel does not supersede, abrogate, eliminate, or fundamentally alter generic nationalism," he writes in the introduction; "it assumes and completes it."[13]

I suspect that if Wolfe and I sat down with a thermos of coffee between us, we could find common ground about several matters of significance. His insistence that nations usually rely on a people's shared ethnicity is both discomfiting and basically true; the United States is an experiment, as we often say, precisely to the degree that it was founded on a shared philosophy rather than ethnicity.[14] I also have to agree with Wolfe that the much-maligned distinction between in-groups and out-groups is literally required for the existence of any community whatsoever since that distinction marks the boundary, and therefore the identity, of any thinkable community.[15] Wolfe further assumes that people have an inborn preference for people who are similar to them, and this translates into a natural love for our homeland and those who hail from it. Distrust of those who differ from us in language or ethnicity is just the photo negative of this preference. Most of us will find this claim unsettling, even disturbing. But few will need to check the consensus in the social sciences to know he is right.[16] I, for one, can even sign on with Wolfe's implied indictment that the liberal order has always been toxic to Christianity—though we would fiercely disagree about why.

But in *The Case for Christian Nationalism*, one fundamental error leads Wolfe to misunderstand the significance of these insights. The error is that, like so many of us, he sees America and not the church of Jesus Christ as his primary community. His gospel is "another gospel," the gospel of America, not the gospel of Jesus Christ. In fact, every other important error he makes is downstream of this one.

Signs of trouble emerge immediately in Wolfe's book. He begins with a long speculative foray into natural theology, which in this case means considering what society and human relationships would be like if there had never been a fall. Such a counterfactual exercise might seem odd, and it is. I would call it unwise at best. To be sure, many theologians, particularly those who lived before the modern era, drew conclusions about the unsullied *imago dei*, how humans were originally meant to be. But few even among the Reformed scholastics that show up everywhere in *The Case for Christian Nationalism* took this train of reasoning all that far. Wolfe admits that "no Christian writer (of which I'm aware) has sought to provide a systematic treatment of human sociality that shows continuity and discontinuity between these [fallen and unfallen] states."[17]

That should have been his first indication that human thought "can't get there from here," at least apart from what is revealed to us in Christ. But Wolfe's reason for setting out in this treacherous direction quickly comes clear. Presenting his conclusions about pre-fall human sociality with breathtaking self-confidence, Wolfe then tries to ground his political theology in the created order, a political theology that blesses the Christian's "dominion mandate" (wrung from Gen. 1:28), the patriarchal family, social hierarchy of many sorts, "martial virtue," and, of course, nationalism. This in turn allows him to draw what seem to be logical inferences about contemporary politics and ethics.

Take an example fundamental to Wolfe's argument. The geographical separateness of human beings and therefore nations are, Wolfe argues, part of the created order. If nations are a part of the created order, they are ordained by God. That also means that God ordained their distinctiveness. But immigrants threaten a people's distinctiveness. Therefore, restrictions on immigration and tight controls on noncitizens can and should be enacted by nation states, even and perhaps especially by those who call themselves "Christian nations." This goes even for immigrants who are fellow Christians but do not share a nation's culture and ethnicity.

> My view is that the principle of exclusion, which is necessary for a people's complete good, morally permits a Christian nation to deny immigration to Christian foreigners. Christian nations are not required to exclude them, but they can in principle.
>
> To demonstrate this, we should first recognize that fellow Christians, regardless of nationality, are united *spiritually*, as fellow members of the kingdom of God. This is chiefly a heavenly or eschatological relation, made

possible by grace, not nature. . . . Thus, all Christians
share in the highest good—all being spiritually united to
Christ—and thus have a spiritual brotherhood. But this
brotherhood—being fit for a *heavenly* kingdom—is wholly
inadequate as to its kind for cooperating to procure the
full range of goods necessary for living well in this world.
Spiritual brotherhood is a common salvation in Christ, an
orientation to heaven, a common interest in the sacred
things for eternal life, and spiritual unity in the worship
of God. But something as basic as a common language,
by which we could cooperate and belong together in the
same place, is absent from spiritual brotherhood. . . . We
cannot ground civic brotherhood on spiritual brotherhood. It simply doesn't work, no matter how much modern sentiment you place on spiritual unity.[18]

Here Wolfe finds himself in a precarious theological position. He finds himself in such a place because, when it comes
to the theological justifications for his political beliefs, he
never reasons from the life of Jesus and the New Testament's
apostolic witness. Which means, despite the caveats he offers
in the above passage, he sees the church as a political non-
entity, a place of purely spiritual instruction (whatever that
could mean).

The church, as Wolfe realizes, lives the politics of the
coming kingdom, but those politics, he writes, are "wholly
inadequate . . . for living well in this world." Talking about
and looking forward to the kingdom proclaimed by the
church is one thing. We should do that. Setting out to *actually live it* politically, on the other hand, is just irresponsible.
And so we find Wolfe calling his political project Christian

nationalism while managing to leave Christ completely out of the equation.

Note that living the politics of the kingdom is not the same thing as perfectionism. We Christians sin. We miss the mark. That is a fact, and nothing this side of the consummation of all things will eradicate sin from our lives entirely. The problem here is not that Wolfe admits that Christians will sin. Instead, it is about the practical orientation he advocates. He wants Christians to focus on civic brotherhood *now*, make the nation our primary political community *now*, and in doing so somehow also prepare ourselves for a heaven in which we live under a very different polity. In this way, it becomes clear that the results of Wolfe's program would look less like the church taking charge of the nation than colonization of the church by the world.

Wolfe's speculation about unfallen sociality, then, is not the root cause of his errors. But he uses the conclusions of his speculation to justify leaving pivotal parts out of the Christian story, the most obvious parts being the birth of the church at Pentecost, Paul's arguments about justification, and the Jerusalem council. Not one of these biblical moments can be left out of an adequate political theology, and it is worth lingering over them to clearly see the effects of Wolfe's disclusions.

Take Pentecost first. Early believers experienced it as the overcoming of the judgment of God carried out at the tower of Babel; the nascent community was knit together through the overcoming of language differences. Because the Spirit had brought them together, the new believers were closer to one another *politically* than they were to those in their ethnic or language group.

The consequences of Pentecost, which we speak of as the birth of the church, did not go undebated as if the matter were merely about individual salvation and had no political consequences. Paul's entire discussion of justification and the council of Jerusalem in Acts 15 involve the question of whether cultural differences between Jew and gentile should factor into how Christians live together. Why was circumcision such a big deal if not because it functioned as a cultural boundary marker to distinguish the Jews, the people of God, from gentiles? Rejecting circumcision and the food laws amounted to a rejection of Israeli exceptionalism. Perhaps it felt like being next to someone refusing to stand for or say the Pledge of Allegiance, and the fact is that the early Christian movement did pose a fatal threat to the Jewish nationalist commitments held by some of its members. No wonder emotions boiled over in these discussions.

Nevertheless, despite these believers' prior commitments to their nation and their people, we can still hear the early church's resounding "No!" to the primacy of nations and cultures echo down to us out of the deep past. "We believe," Peter told the church gathered at the Jerusalem council, "it is through the grace of our Lord Jesus that we are saved, just as they are." The implications of this truth were undeniable and probably frightening to Peter's audience: *they were now more bound to gentile Christians than to their fellow Jews. And their countrymen might well see this commitment as treason.*

Paul had precisely the same message for the Galatian people in what is now central Turkey: "There is neither Jew nor Greek, slave nor free, male nor female, for you are all one in Christ Jesus" (Gal. 3:28). The emergence of the church meant for the first Christians that *their nations or ethnic peoples were no longer their primary political community.* Now the church was their community, the community that gave its allegiance to Christ rather than Caesar and whose political life together simply *is* discipleship to him. As Peter said, "you are a chosen people, a royal priesthood, a holy nation, a people belonging to God, that you may declare the praises of him who called you out of darkness into his wonderful light. Once you were not a people, but now you are the people of God; once you had not received mercy, but now you have received mercy" (1 Pet. 2:9–10).

Like John Calvin and many other Protestants, Wolfe emphasizes that the true church is invisible. Not everyone who occupies a pew on Sunday morning has the Spirit, and, just perhaps, not everyone removed from the assembly of the faithful lacks faith. The election of God, not good deeds, brings human beings into the kingdom. Amen, I say. But what we most certainly cannot do with this key theological truth is extend its logic to say that the church's life in the world has no relationship to its election. That claim is false and has done untold damage among evangelical believers.

What's more, the new community Peter was writing about was anything but invisible. Think about it. Before the coming of Christ, the chosen people, the royal priesthood, and the holy nation had been ethnic Israel (Deut. 7:6), a very much visible body that was quite serious about the space it took up in the world.[19] The controversy in the early church about non-Jews makes zero sense if the first Christians thought true religion was purely internal, metaphysical, and just between you and God, and not also very much *political*.

Christians have always said that the Spirit gathers the church as a community and orients the church *politically* to the word of God. If tares turn up among the wheat, well-behaved unbelievers among the faithful, or even wolves among the sheep, we must nevertheless always expect that Christ will lead his church. Even when we rebel, he reorients us as a community to our communal good, himself. That is, he calls us to repentance.

Has any other reality—whether the nation, an ideology, or any other good—become your "ultimate concern"? Then repentance is in order. *Metanoia*, the Greek word for repentance, means "change your mind." So change your mind! Reorient your mind and your life *politically* toward Christ. But what if your Christian community's life is directed toward nation, ideology, or some other good rather than the gospel? Then your community is not a church in the full sense of the word. The Spirit is not the animating force in your life together and the word is not your political orientation. Wolfe wants a national church for the United States that preaches and practices Christian nationalism; therefore, his "church" would not be a church in the full sense of the word.

Wolfe is hardly alone in longing for this sort of "church" and this sort of "gospel." Dutch Sheets, a charismatic preacher, YouTuber, and avowed theocrat, criticizes evangelicals for discipling individuals but not "discipling nations."[20] Certain right-wing circles in the Catholic church have fallen for what is called integralism, the idea that the church and modern societies should be "integrated." Then there's Doug Wilson, a classical-education advocate, Reformed theonomist, and, in his own words, a "paleo-confederate."[21] Examples are a dime a dozen, and in every case, the Christian nationalist's claim to radical gospel-centeredness turns out upon closer inspection to really be passion for a certain conservative view of what America should be: nineteenth-century America, especially the South; 1950s suburban America; or, in the case of some integralists, a modern America suddenly and improbably merged with medieval Christendom.

Such religious reveries never end with the church ruling the nation. They end with the colonization of the church by the nation. Good intentions do nothing to alter the inevitable outcome of such promethean projects, these Christian towers of Babel. As Karl Barth put it, "This theocratic dream comes abruptly to an end, of course, when we discover that it is the Devil who approaches Jesus and offers Him all the kingdoms of this world."[22]

Those less plugged into Twitter are probably thinking of the Jerry Falwells (both Jr. and Sr.), Franklin Graham, or other evangelical culture warriors like Eric Metaxas. Perhaps you feel that these men differ profoundly from Wolfe and his ilk and lumping them together is deceptive. They, by contrast, reject theocracy. They embrace religious freedom. Grouping them with Wolfe is just a typical liberal move designed to tar and feather good, faithful people.

Au contraire. Such men and women also make Wolfe's move. They just make it less consistently. Sure, the result for the nation might be different, but that, frankly, is a secondary matter. In comparison with what happens in the church, it's small potatoes. As we have seen, culture-warrior Christianity is catastrophic for the church: another gospel, a false gospel, dethrones the good news about Jesus Christ, reorienting the church politically toward the nation.

An example taken at random from Falwell Sr. can make this point for me. That the founder of Moral Majority preached the gospel of America every bit as fervently as his anti-pluralist allies comes across clear as day in a talk given at the Cleveland City Club on March 26, 1982:

> I'm often asked to justify how as a minister of the gospel
> I can support President Reagan's policy in El Salvador.
> Well, I happen to believe that freedom in Central Amer-
> ica impacts upon freedom in North America.... We so
> quickly forget that the Soviet goal is not Cuba or Nicara-
> gua, both now in the Soviet camp, but world conquest....
> Well, I enjoy freedom. So as a minister of the gospel I
> speak out against those things, and I personally feel that
> freedom is the basic moral issue of all issues.[23]

"So," Falwell tells his audience, "Mr. Reagan's enemies are
my enemies. They're yours too."

Forget for a moment that Falwell publicly supported US-
backed death squads that killed Archbishop Oscar Romero
and thousands of others. Forget that the Salvadoran campe-
sinos murdered by their government cared nothing for Soviet
goals or the appropriation of the means of production. Look
at the actual words Falwell used. He apparently believed that
his status as a "minister of the gospel" should lead him to
speak against the Soviet Union and for the American-style
"freedom" of liberal democracy and capitalism.

*Why?* Why should the life, death, and resurrection of Jesus
Christ and the Spirit-driven life of the community he has
formed lead Falwell to cheerlead for liberal democracy and
capitalism? What would make him think that when St. Paul
said, "It is for freedom that Christ has set us free," the apostle
meant freedom to shop, freedom to be comfortable, *or even
freedom from governmental oppression?* How could the gospel
lead Falwell to say, "Mr. Reagan's enemies are my enemies"?
For anyone with eyes to see and ears to hear, Falwell's argument is complete and utter nonsense—unless he too, like

Wolfe and today's Trump strategists, was preaching the gospel of America rather than the gospel of Jesus Christ.

Many younger evangelicals, fed up with Moral Majority politics, have moved to the left, taken up libertarianism, or moved to the hard right. Many gave up practicing their faith in public altogether and put their energy into other causes. But these shifts miss the heart of the evangelical crisis. After all, putting another American gospel in the place of Falwell's will get evangelicalism to exactly the same place. The liberal internationalist gospel, the White nationalist gospel, the DEI gospel, the ever-popular gospel of poor, forgotten Middle America—all of them proclaim that the business of Christians is to save the nation or, perhaps, the world, and all of them end in the colonization of the church by the world and its business.[24] But the business of Christians isn't to save America or any particular vision of America. The business of Christians is to follow Jesus together as the people of God in public in a way that points those who do not believe toward their master. This does not mean withdrawing from the world. Despite the angst that plagued Billy Graham after Nixon, it may not even mean withdrawing from politics. But it emphatically does mean living by a wholly other script, seeing our lives as a part of a history far more important than America's history: the unfolding drama of God with his people that culminated in Jesus's life, death, and resurrection.

As you finish this chapter, you might be thinking, "I still don't get it. What do you mean by 'another gospel'? How in practice is evangelicalism in America missing the mark?" That's the right question. Two tasks remain for me in this short book that may help answer it.

We must, above all, look to the life of Jesus. No manual for Christian political action can be constructed out of these stories, but we will find in them the outlines of a politics that has been practiced by a few in every age of the church. Before we get there, however, an example from further afield seems in order. We Americans live and breathe the gospel of America. It's so familiar, many of us fail to recognize it unless someone points it out. A less familiar example of Christian nationalism, one from a different nation, may help clarify just what the life of the church might look like under Wolfe's "Christian prince" and, just maybe, what life is like in our evangelical churches now.

# 4

# PUTIN'S CHRISTIAN NATIONALISM

Vladimir Vladimirovich Putin stood silent before the stone of anointing, the slab of rock where the body of Jesus is said to have been prepared for burial. His retinue and the Russian priest tasked with serving as his guide let him alone. It was April 2005, just before Eastern Orthodox Easter, and though he was in the region for highly anticipated meetings with Palestinian President Mahmud Abbas and Israeli Prime Minister Ariel Sharon, the president gave off the air of a pilgrim. The former KGB agent and head of the FSB had come to the Church of the Holy Sepulchre before he did anything else.[1]

After some time, Putin disappeared alone into the small shrine marking Jesus's tomb. When he emerged after quite a long while, he climbed the stairway to the rock of Golgotha, where he knelt and prayed. Rising, he lit a candle and looked as if he would leave. But suddenly, to everyone's surprise, he turned back and fell to his knees again at the foot of the cross.

This was not Putin's first pilgrimage, nor would it be his last. The political scientist Dmitry Adamsky has claimed with some credibility that Putin "has exploited every opportunity to undergo pilgrim experiences, some of them hardly publicized."[2] And he is far from alone among Russian elites. Today those who want access to the president and other high-ranking officials often find that traditional Russian Orthodox faith is the Kremlin's preferred currency. Across Russia big business and elite men vying for government contracts are buying up relics from abroad, building churches and chapels, and even booking a weekend at the monasteries of Mount Athos in Greece. Military clergy, who were few and basically powerless before the start of Putin's (then unconstitutional) third term in 2012, have rapidly gained influence, and churches and chapels built for servicemen have popped up around military sites.[3] Before the war, three new churches were being built in Russia every day.[4] Nearly ten thousand have been built since 2010.

The days of Soviet atheism are long gone. The last thirty years have seen a distinctively Russian form of Christian nationalism gradually take hold among everyone from elite Muscovites to the rural poor. Many seem to feel Moscow has succeeded Rome and Byzantium as the seat of Christendom. Brutalist architecture is out; onion domes and icons are in. So is nostalgia for the tsars and the Russian Empire. Or, to put the matter more precisely, nowadays being Christian and making the Russian Empire great again seem to many Russians to be almost the same thing. In the seventeen years after the fall of the Soviet Union, the share of Russian adults identifying as Orthodox rose from 31 percent to 72 percent.[5] Today it is 81 percent. Yet only a fraction of those who see themselves as Orthodox believe Orthodox doctrine, and only a fraction of that number (perhaps

6 percent of the populace) darken the door of a church more than occasionally.

In 2009 Patriarch Kirill, who had already been a force in national politics, took the helm of the Russian Church, and three years later Putin, tired of his sometimes Western-friendly protégé Dmitry Medvedev keeping his chair warm, settled back into his old Kremlin office. Since then, Putin's personal confessor has become a household name, the media has spotlighted faith with increased regularity, and the anti-Christian tilt of Western culture and politics become part of nearly every Russian politician's stump speeches. Church attendance today, however, actually seems to be slowly decreasing.

Some American evangelicals might respond, "Well, it's a start! Perhaps all this cultural Christianity will open them to the gospel." My response would be, "Why would you think any of this would open Russians to *the gospel* rather than *another gospel*?" I dare say that's exactly the question Saint Paul would ask us.

In fact, we can see the fruits of Russian Orthodox political dominance well enough already. Christian nationalism has not rebuilt the church in Russia after Communism. In fact, the church seems to have been healthier behind the Iron Curtain. The triumphant return of Russian Orthodoxy to the center of Russian public life has not even encouraged peace with Moscow's Orthodox neighbors. On the contrary, we will see that the Christian-nationalist narrative of Russian history may well have motivated Putin's invasion of Ukraine, and we have good reason to think that it could motivate Putin to push his military to the limit—even to the point of deploying tactical nuclear weapons.

Sometimes we cannot see the board in our eye until we see the board in someone else's. To be sure, our spiritual vision has become too weak to help the Russian church with their board. But if we try to understand their spiritual and theological malady, we just might be granted insight into ours. Understanding Russian Christian nationalists' logic about their country's providential history is indispensable if we want to understand the mindset that led Putin to invade, and that means we will need to take a deep dive into Russian history. But along the way, parallels will arise with the histories we evangelicals often tell about the United States. Just how our sight has been obscured by the theology of Christian nationalism will become increasingly clear.

Bring back to mind the picture of Putin emotionally enraptured and kneeling at the foot of the cross. Now juxtapose the image you have in your mind with the images of death and destruction you have seen in reports from the front lines in Ukraine. A man who seems to love Christ; a man in the process of perpetrating the most terrible crime Europe has seen in generations.The two images seem impossible to reconcile until you read an essay Putin published just months before the invasion during the summer of 2021: "On the Historical Unity of Russians and Ukrainians."[6] Ukraine, the Russian president thinks, is not a real nation. It always has been and therefore always should be part of Russia.

The ex-KGB man believes this first and foremost because of a baptism. Vladimir the Great, Prince of Novgorod and Grand Prince of Kyiv, was baptized in AD 988 at Chersonesus in Crimea, the southernmost part of Ukraine. Kievan Rus', a predecessor state to both Ukraine and Russia, had existed for more than a century as a pagan state before Vladimir came to power. Now the elite began to be baptized as Christians, creating what would one day become the most powerful Orthodox church outside Byzantium. So, Putin argues, Ukrainians and Russians were "bound together" from the beginning by "the Orthodox faith." Together they were—and therefore supposedly are—a Christian nation.

Putin and his allies often articulate Russian civil religion in much broader terms to accommodate nonbelievers and Russia's significant Muslim minority. But for the Orthodox majority, this baptism is fundamental. When decoded, it conveys messages as general as "God has a special relationship with Russia" or as specific as "God intended Russia and Ukraine to be one nation" or even "in giving Russia Kyiv and Ukraine, God intended Russia to be a European and geopolitical power."

But a closer look at the history creates intractable problems for this story. Prince Vladimir himself—whom, it is worth noting, Ukrainians have always called Volodymyr (the first name of the current Ukrainian president)—was neither a Russian nor a Ukrainian. He was a Viking. When Vladimir was baptized, Kyiv had already existed for half a millennium, but Moscow, which would become the seed of the Russian empire, would not be founded for another 150 years. Further, Vladimir's baptism was a purely political matter. The baptism that Russians often call the "baptism of Rus'" was done with the understanding that the Byzantine emperor would give Vladimir his sister in marriage. It also happened after he first led pagan attempts to suppress the Christian faith. Whatever the so-called baptism of Rus' was, it was not the baptism of Russia.

Subsequent medieval history helps Putin's case for the unity of Ukraine and Russia even less. Crimea—both the site of the AD 988 baptism and the strategically critical Black Sea peninsula that Russia invaded in 2014—has had numerous rulers, but until recent centuries precisely none of them were Russian. Kievan Rus' claimed but never controlled Crimea. Genghis Khan and the Golden Horde swept through the area in the late thirteenth century, but the khans' political influence remained. The Crimean khanate's people raided Russian lands for centuries, and their faith was Muslim rather than Orthodox. When Russia finally came to control Crimea through negotiations with the declining Ottoman Empire and the hated khanate ceased to exist, it was the eve of the French Revolution.

The thought that Crimea was originally Russian is therefore a modern innovation. But to say so in today's Russia amounts to heresy. To be sure, obsession with Crimea has, at least in the past, involved more than this: for example, lust for its Black Sea deepwater port and elite vacation spots. But today it almost always also involves a passionate Christian nationalism, above all the sort that claims the so-called baptism of Rus' as its origin story. Crimea must be Russian, such Orthodox nationalists feel, because the nation was born there. Putin's essay fits this pattern exactly.

Christian nationalism also moved Putin to take special note of the year 1649. That is the year, he writes, that Zaporozhian Cossacks, a tribal and semi-stateless people of Orthodox faith living in southern Ukraine, appealed to Moscow for help in dealing with religious persecution permitted by the Polish-Lithuanian Commonwealth. He sees this appeal as the unification of Orthodox kindred who were once one people within Kievan Rus', and, in fact, he gets all this history basically right—other than the fact that these Cossacks were most certainly not Russian. For centuries they fought for whoever would give them the better political deal. Occasionally that meant fighting against Russia, especially after the tsar got control of their land. They appealed to Moscow in 1649 because at that time the Polish-Lithuanian Commonwealth dominated the region, and they needed a military and political counterweight. An alliance with Russia served that purpose. Annexation by Russia, which came a generation after the alliance, was greeted not with gratitude for the gift of religious freedom, but by violent resistance.

Putin has here made the same move with Crimea he made with Kyiv; astonishingly, he tried it again with Lithuania. He refers to early Lithuania as Lithuanian Rus' and writes that their faith was Orthodox, thereby creating the sense that they and the areas that were formerly under their control (including Ukraine) are also somehow Russian. In truth, the faith of the Lithuanian elite was pagan longer than anywhere else in Europe, and, along with the Ottomans, they were Russia's main geopolitical rival for centuries. Notice what has happened. For Putin the Orthodox faith is functioning not to bring all people into the one, holy, universal church, but to bring European nations under the Russian banner.

In 1686 Russia finally got ahold of northeastern Ukraine and the city of Kyiv, seven hundred years after Putin believes the Russian and Ukrainian peoples originated as one people. On the cusp of becoming an empire, Russian ambitions were rapidly growing, and possession of the ancient city of Kyiv gave them a foothold in Europe. "The incorporation of the western Russian lands into the single state," Putin writes, "was not merely the result of political and diplomatic decisions. It was underlain by the common faith, shared cultural traditions, and . . . language similarity." To translate Putin from politico-speak into straight talk, the Orthodox faith shared by Ukrainians and Russians justified the taking of Kyiv by force. After all, religion along with tradition and language is the glue that holds peoples together; spiritually speaking, this ancient city's inhabitants were Russian no matter what their rulers or the people themselves said at the time.

But that glue never had the strength Russian Christian nationalists like to believe. Crimean Tatars and their Muslim faith, Uniate Catholics who looked to Rome rather than Constantinople, and much of western Ukraine were far from fully Russified when tensions began rising in the late nineteenth century between the Austrian Hapsburgs and Moscow. This is why in the years before World War I, the Hapsburgs, then rulers of southwest Ukraine, could hamstring Russia by allowing and even nurturing Ukrainian nationalism.[7] Why did they think stoking pro-Ukrainian sentiment in their own territories would make the same thing happen in Russian-controlled territory? Because they knew there was already Ukrainian national feeling there to nurture.

The Soviets too recognized Ukrainian nationality, which is why Stalin prioritized Ukrainization. That term meant encouraging local officials to speak Ukrainian, teaching Ukrainian history, and generally supporting Ukrainian culture. Putin claims that this misguided Soviet policy "played a major role in the development and consolidation of the Ukrainian culture, language and identity," that the Soviets disrupted the unity of Russia and Ukraine that existed under the tsars. But the Soviets had no reason to develop nationalisms that did not already exist. Putin's narrative about Stalin's

Ukraine policy is one more just-so story; its shape is determined by the moral that Ukraine and Russia are one.[8]

We should keep in mind, however, that this narrative functions not just to rationalize a land grab but to make sense of Russia's place in the post-Soviet world. The narrative works so well because it binds Russian national identity inextricably to Orthodox religion. That is not an indictment of Russian Orthodoxy as a whole, but a description of how Orthodoxy functions within the Russian nationalist story. As all civil religions do, Orthodoxy gives the Russian nationalist story divine imprimatur. It inculcates faith in the nation's transcendent goodness primarily through stories of providential intervention at critical points in the nation's history. Such collective "memories" create national identity and counteract other stories that might inculcate disloyalty—which means that preservation of faith in those stories and the forging of new ones is quite literally a matter of national security.

We could hardly ask for a clearer example than the years immediately before and after the collapse of the USSR. Even before *glasnost* (openness), Orthodoxy began moving in to fill the widening cracks in the edifice of Russian national identity that Communism could no longer fill. In 1988, the thousand-year anniversary of the baptism of Rus' became a major national event throughout the Soviet Union. After Gorbachev's resignation and the formation of the Commonwealth of Independent States, the Orthodox hierarchy moved quickly to forge relationships with major institutions, especially the military. History suddenly became quite unpredictable.[9] Various myths arose that claimed Stalin himself and other major figures from the Great Patriotic War (World War II) were secretly Orthodox. Major publications argued that God's miraculous intervention and the people's faith held back the Nazis from Moscow and later Stalingrad. As the decade went on, many Russian elite began to feel that to go forward they must go back, back to the hand-in-glove relationship the church often had with the tsar before the Bolsheviks. Being a good Orthodox Christian and being a good Russian, it was increasingly felt, amounted to the same thing.

A talk given by Kirill, who then had the title of metropolitan, to the mostly non-Christian senior commanders of the Commonwealth of Independent States armed forces in 1994 shows us the way the wind was blowing. He argued that the church had a responsibility to provide not just ethical guidance for individual officers and conscripts, but a moral groundwork for the military as a whole. Then he brought up the baptism of AD 988. He did this, Dmitry Adamsky writes, to emphasize "the importance of the faith-based geopolitical solidarity of the thousand-year-old communality of nations."[10] "What will happen," Kirill asked, "if father and son swear an oath of allegiance to different states? What will happen if [Russia and Ukraine], God forbid, decide to resolve their issues with arms?" Avoiding war would necessarily involve strengthening Orthodoxy as part of both countries' national identity.

But consider what would happen if his listeners adopted Kirill's vision. The head of the Ukrainian church was then the patriarch in Moscow. There was no separate Ukrainian church. There was only the Russian church, and that meant for Kirill that a fundamental part of Ukrainian national identity must be its spiritual orientation toward Russia. The man who would become patriarch is only a short step away from saying that to avoid war Ukraine must be unified (spiritually and culturally if not politically) with Russia.

An implicit threat of aggression lurked here no matter what the West or NATO did. Discussion of Ukraine's value to imperial powers often focuses on its Black Sea ports, rich farmland (hence the nickname "the breadbasket of Europe"), or the heavy industry in the eastern provinces that was so valuable during the Soviet era. But Kirill never mentions these, and today Putin's obsession with Ukraine is more or less unconnected to such economic and military advantages. Rather, it involves Vladimir the Great's baptism and the Russian national myths that later grew up around it. Since 1991, the Russian church has sought to connect "Holy Rus'" and "Russian civilization's values" in the national consciousness, and they seem to have succeeded. Before the Bolsheviks took power, Orthodox civil religion served to buttress the tsar's imperial government. Now we have a new tsar, one as devoted, or more so, to the nationalist Orthodox narrative than the tsars of old. Ukraine going its own way would mean the disintegration of the story he and many in his nation now live by.

All this makes intelligible the Russian response to a recent painful affair within the larger Orthodox church. In January 2019 Patriarch Bartholomew, the Ecumenical Patriarch, allowed the Ukrainian Orthodox Church to separate from the Russian Orthodox Church and made it accountable to his church in Constantinople (Istanbul) instead. The Russian church immediately severed ties with Constantinople and later broke communion with several other major branches of Orthodoxy, initiating the greatest schism among Christians in more than three hundred years. The wider church had effectively dismissed Russia's claim to Ukraine; Russia and its church could either let go of Ukraine and their Christian-nationalist narrative or dismiss the rest of the body of Christ. They chose the latter.

Few in the West have considered the role the 2018 schism played in Putin's decision to invade, but if the essay he wrote is any clue, it was hardly negligible. Putin was prepared to absorb hundreds of thousands of Russian casualties and a catastrophic economic contraction because this war, as he said in the days after the invasion, is about "the preservation of Russia." He sees it as a fight for the nation's soul. That soul is Orthodox, and its ancestral home is Crimea. It is, as Putin said in 2015, of "invaluable civilizational and sacral importance for Russia, like the Temple Mount in Jerusalem for the followers of Islam and Judaism."[11] Russia cannot be Russia without it.

This is why seeing the war primarily as a clash of great powers (NATO and Russia) is a mistake. If that were so, we could expect Putin to act in a rational and self-interested manner. Once it became clear that Russia was losing more than it gained by continuing the war, he would have withdrawn his forces. But that point came and went almost immediately after the war began. Ukraine is a nation with serious social problems, and its heavy industry and deepwater port no longer provide the advantages they did a century ago. "Ukraine was, is, and always will be important to Russia," Dominic Lieven writes, "but . . . imagining that Russia will once again be a great empire if it reabsorbs the east Ukrainian rust belt is moonshine. Ukraine is no longer at the heart of European geopolitics, and Europe is no longer at the center of the world."[12]

Putin knows this. He knows taking Ukraine would hardly put him on par with the United States or Europe. Instead, Putin's reasons for continuing to prosecute this war are all about Christian nationalism and Russian identity. This is why we cannot expect the introduction of Western tanks, which is beginning as I write these words, to seriously change Putin's calculus. Western policymakers should believe the normally cautious Putin willing to deploy tactical nuclear weapons to keep a foothold in Ukraine, particularly if Ukrainian forces jeopardize his hold on Crimea. And if he does give such an order, we should expect those in the military hierarchy to carry it out.

Two reasons for this come to mind: the fundamental role of nuclear weapons in Putin's view of Russian defense and the influence of Orthodoxy within the culture of nuclear officers and developers. After a 2007 speech, a journalist asked Putin about the places of Orthodoxy and nuclear weapons in Russia. A murmur of laughter ran through the room when he responded that the "themes were closely interlinked." The rest of his answer, however, made it clear that he was quite serious.

> Traditional confessions and the nuclear shield are those components that strengthen Russian statehood and create the necessary preconditions for providing the state's internal and external security. Therefore, a clear conclusion can be drawn, about how the state should relate, today and in the future, to the one and to the other.[13]

Here, Adamsky writes, Putin had "communicated his credo." Orthodoxy provides the cultural and ideological foundation for the state, what he calls its internal security. The nuclear program complements Orthodoxy by providing external security, the ultimate military trump card that every other nation on the planet knows Russia possesses. One can draw Putin's "clear conclusion" only by realizing these "themes were closely interlinked": that a nuclear response is called for when an external power tries to destroy Russia's internal security as defined by Russian Orthodox Christian nationalism. Crimea's central role in the Russian Christian-nationalist narrative should lead us to expect a nuclear response if Ukrainian forces launch a successful offensive against Sevastopol or cut off Russian forces in Crimea from the Russian mainland.

The nuclear forces will be ready. Nationalist Russian Orthodoxy, like American civil religion, has always made saints out of those who defend the fatherland, and in the post-Soviet era of Russian weakness, the nation's nuclear arsenal became critical in the national psyche. Not surprisingly, then, the nuclear branch is today the most aggressively consecrated and catechized branch in the entire armed forces. The Soviets established a major nuclear research facility in the old Sarov Monastery three hundred miles east of Moscow that housed the relics of Saint Seraphim Sarovsky. They did so in part to wipe out the memory of this saint. Putin kept them there to do the opposite. Sarovsky became the patron saint of Russian nuclear-weapon developers, who often note that Seraphim in Hebrew means "burning ones."[14] Their work to defend Russia, it is felt, is nothing short of holy.

Would Russians continue to back their new tsar if he broke the nuclear taboo? It's hardly possible to draw firm conclusions, but we must at least take into account the rhetoric about Ukraine being deployed by Russian talking heads. Yes, in the first months of the war they claimed the Zelensky regime were neo-Nazis, and they called their "special military operation" "denazification." Such rhetoric aimed to drum up support for the war by connecting it with a moment in which Russia (or the Soviet Union) was fighting for its very existence: the "Great Patriotic War" against Hitler. It worked, at least to some degree. Would it shield Putin from criticism and possible attempts on his life if he pushed the big red button? Let's just say he would be a fool to count on it.

Perhaps this is why another, more up-to-date epithet came into use among some Russian media personalities and regime supporters. Taking the Kremlin's lead, they have begun calling Ukraine and its allies satanic. Unlike the "denazification" story, more than cynicism motivates the production of this propaganda. We can bet that not a few purveyors of this rhetoric really believe what they're saying, that the Russian forces fight "not against flesh and blood, but against the rulers, against the authorities, against the powers of this dark world and against the spiritual forces of evil in the heavenly realms" (Eph. 6:12).

In his September 2022 speech announcing Russia's annexation of four regions of eastern Ukraine, Putin himself framed the invasion in terms of a wider culture war against the United States, the "satanic" power behind the transgender movement.[15] A few weeks later Aleksey Pavlov, assistant secretary of the Russian Security Council, wrote an article calling for the "complete de-Satanization" of Kiev, saying that Satanism, a religion "officially registered in the United States," had "spread across Ukraine." "Is it any wonder that in 2015 in Kiev a group of pagans broke and desecrated a worship cross erected for the 1000th anniversary of the repose of the Holy Equal-to-the-Apostles Grand Duke Vladimir, the Baptist of Rus'?" he asked.[16] Even Dmitry Medvedev then decided to drop his open, tech-friendly image for full-on Christian nationalism. A few weeks later, during a speech in Saint Petersburg, he said that Russia's mission was to "stop the supreme ruler of Hell, whatever name he uses" and that Russia had the ability to "send all our enemies to fiery Gehenna." While the West and Ukrainians lie like Satan, the father of lies, Medvedev said, "our weapon is the truth."[17]

None of this is new. Russian media outlets dubbed their enemies satanic before the internationalization of the transgender movement. After the invasion of Crimea in 2014, Russian state media tried to link the Ukrainian prime minister as well as the head of parliament Oleksandr Turchynov (a Baptist) to a Satan-worshipping sect.[18]

And further, like in America, none of this is confined to churchgoers. Non-Christians and even adherents of other religions sometimes make the most fervent Christian nationalists. One example is Apti Aloudinov, the head of Chechen forces and a Muslim, who called the West and the LGBTQ movement "Satanic" on state TV. "During all of my youth, I've been preparing for this war we see today," he said. "This is a holy war our saints and elders spoke of. I grew up on this." Then he pivoted to his love for Russia, a nation that many of his fellow Chechens have hated as an imperialist presence in their land.

> I will tell you one thing: I praise the Most High that I live in Russia today. I praise the Most High that this country is headed by Vladimir Vladimirovich Putin because he is the man that refused to accept so-called European values. In fact, those are Satanist values that are imposed on the entire world. I'm grateful for him that he remains that

person that adheres to the values and [that] this nation is moving on the path of the Most High. We are not under the flags of the LGBT, and as long as he's alive, we won't be under those flags.

Let me go back and say why I think this is a holy war and why I believe we will certainly win this war. Everything that we see today, this NATO bloc and all that, when I was reading the Islamic scriptures and Christian Scriptures—I studied the Bible, the Qur'an, and Torah. I studied everything that could be studied. From all these Scriptures, I know we're facing the war against the devil's army . . . the antichrist. And I'm being asked, "What makes you think that you are the army that will confront the army of the antichrist?" Many were surprised when I said, "[The army of my fellow largely Muslim Chechen fighters] is the army of Jesus because we wait for the coming of Christ more than anyone. But [we are] not the only one. All units and forces fighting on the side of Russia are the army of Jesus.[19]

This, the citizens of Russia are meant to understand, is the last battle, the decisive moment in history when, despite how things look, good will finally triumph over evil. Which is why Russians must understand who it is they fight. "Underneath this democracy of America, the main enemy of mankind, and Europe, the minion of the NATO bloc, which carries within it everything that is Satanic—this is the army of the antichrist."

Even in America, some evangelicals have begun to think there's a certain amount of truth in what Putin, the Kremlin, and Russian state television say about Ukraine and the West and, if so, that he must have the right approach in using military force. So let us set the record straight. Vladimir Putin, who has become increasingly isolated even from formerly close advisors, made the decision to invade almost single-handedly. He continues to make this choice, a choice that has cost more than a quarter million people their lives. Ukraine did nothing to make this choice sensible or even rational from the perspective of power politics. The US or Europe or Ukraine did not begin this war. Vladimir Putin did.

But let us say for the sake of argument that Putin is right. Protecting Russia from American values or George Soros's Open Society (name your favorite conspiracy theory here) or the LGBT movement may well have been on Putin's mind, so let us be generous and say the encroachment of the West is actually happening in precisely the ways he imagines. He invaded Crimea in 2014 immediately after the Euromaidan protests in Kyiv, protests that participants hoped would shift Ukraine out of Russia's sphere of influence and closer to Europe. In a limited sense, that would indeed have brought American power to Russia's very borders—and just perhaps, ever increasing doses of American and Western culture. Say then that the EU or even NATO is in Ukraine's future if Putin does nothing. Say, for the sake of argument, that may eventually mean feminism, gay marriage, and trans rights and that these are all grave social evils. Does this mean that as a professing Christian Vladimir Putin was right to invade Ukraine?

Of course not! Set aside international norms and the offensive rather than defensive nature of Russia's war. Set aside even the Christian tradition of just war theory that goes back to Augustine. The fact that all of us cannot immediately answer this question with an unequivocal "No!" to Putin's horrifying choice demonstrates that we do not understand the nature of the church or the gospel that the church proclaims.

Putin, his yes-men, and many in the Russian Orthodox hierarchy chose Russia over the body of Christ. They decided that the future they wanted to build was more important than what God has and will build. They decided that the political community of the nation was more important than the political community joined together in the flesh of Christ. In so deciding, they put themselves in danger of blaspheming the Spirit. They, not the Ukrainians, broke communion with their brothers and sisters when the Patriarch of Constantinople granted Ukraine its own church in 2019. They then destroyed the property, institutions, and lives of those they called brothers and sisters in the faith and agreed together to lie about their reasons for doing it. The rejection of the one, universal church implied by this war tells us that the revival of faith in Russia is not orthodox (little *o*) even if it is Orthodox, that it propagates *another* gospel—not the gospel of Jesus Christ and his kingdom, but the gospel of the greatness of Russia.

This false gospel is the gospel of Christian nationalism, and, as it always does, the rending of the church's unity provides our first clue to its presence. But it rarely comes without unholy company. Power lust—a faithless sense that we must take control or the world will go to hell—almost always shows up too, and that should hardly surprise us. Nation-states defend their borders and police their interiors using overwhelming violence. That is just the way nations work. So if our primary political community is the nation, we will have a very difficult time having the mind of Christ (Phil. 2:5–11). Being a people that empty ourselves by taking the political stance of a servant toward friend and enemy alike will appear unintelligible at best. Instead, we will tend to think and act in terms of violence and lust for power—and then just baptize *that* as Christian.

The contemporary Russian case is no different. In April 2023 Patriarch Kirill called fighting for Russia "the greatest duty and a holy deed," a sentence that is nothing short of assault on the body of Christ.[20] He has left antiwar clerics and Christian critics of the hierarchy vulnerable to persecution for speaking out, for example, about the incredible brutality of the Wagner Group contractors and their glorification in Russian pop culture.[21] And then, almost unimaginably, he has called the murder of his Ukrainian brothers and sisters in Christ "holy." Presumably Kirill took this tack with the best of intentions. We can only assume that he too believes God is on Russia's side. But how, we must ask, could he have become so deluded?

Because at some point Kirill bought into a false gospel, the gospel of Russia. His knack for realpolitik brought the ecclesial powers that be into line with an establishment longing for national glory. The gospel he seems to live has invited the colonization of the Russian Orthodox Church by the nation, its hopes, and its habitual ways of thinking. His imagination has been captured by the wrong narratives, his hope and desire set on the wrong objects.

This could, of course, happen to any of us. If Satan disguises himself as an angel of light, his favorite disguise in many parts of the world might involve a flag pin and rhetoric about the enemies of the people. The US is no exception.

It is a seductive ideology. I know because I myself was seduced by it.

As a boy I had a recurring dream: the Soviets were invading. A sudden gloom falls over the cornfields that surround my parents' house and the church next door where my father served as pastor. Though my rural west Michigan hometown would hardly interest military strategists, the sky is filled with Soviet MiGs.

I fly down the driveway, dodging bullets, heading for the empty, dilapidated barn in which my brothers and I sometimes played and cut ourselves on rusty nails and old glass. I leap into the cockpit of my own, child-sized plane, a single-engine machine that looked something like a miniature World War II-era Grumman Bearcat. I fire it up, and immediately I'm in a dogfight. Some nights I take a few bullets; usually, I make my way home unscathed. But every time I give those commies something to remember me by. I take out a group of planes about to strafe my house (the school, by contrast, could go up in flames). Or I elude a couple fighters that pick up my tail and then turn the tables on them. Often, I take out a bomber headed toward town, and leave debris—but, of course, no bodies—strewn over the fields.

The Berlin Wall fell when I was seven. The USSR had probably already ceased to exist when my subconscious conjured up these gratifying dreams. Given that background, you might wonder if they were inspired by patriotic passions in my childhood home. I doubt that's the case. My parents had no military background and no overt nationalist bent, and, other than an American flag in the corner of the stage that caused some bitter conflicts over the years, neither did the church in which I was raised.

Nevertheless, somewhere along the line my imagination had been colonized. I had no clear sense that glorying in the destruction of America's enemies might be incompatible with the gospel. Kirill might well have had a reoccurring dream like mine as a child, only in reverse. As someone born toward the end of the Stalin era, that would have been understandable. But now we see the fruit of such a colonized imagination: the Russian patriarch has repeatedly felt it necessary to publicly baptize evil so that good might result. The good he seeks is the glorification of the nation and thereby the well-being of the Russian people. We might just call that nationalism. Yet the fruits of his labor have turned out to be poison, and everyone who is willing, Christian or not, can see it.

# 5

# A GOSPEL POLITICS

"Again, the devil took him to a very high mountain and showed him all the kingdoms of the world and their splendor; and he said to him, 'All these I will give you, if you will bow down and worship me'" (Matt. 4:8–9 NRSV).

Hold Jesus's form in your mind's eye as he looks down from that windswept crag. The frailty and suffering inherent in the human condition was his as well as the power and authority of the divine nature. Ask yourself, what went through his mind when Satan made this offer?

> You know, the inter-kingdom community is on the cusp of world-changing forward progress. I could institute democratic rule, establish security to ensure economic growth over the long term, and put the right experts in place to establish institutional fidelity and longevity. Maybe I eventually build myself a nice, but not lavish house on the Mediterranean and an apartment in Jerusalem upscale enough to host visiting dignitaries. Once I'd changed cultural expectations about transitions of power and human rights, raised educational standards, and rooted out corruption

*in local governments, I could have a quiet retirement with family and friends. Maybe it would make pragmatic sense to take Satan up on his offer.*

Now that I put it in writing, that sounds stupid, doesn't it? Perhaps something more "kenotic":

*Well, Satan, that looks awfully nice. But, look, I don't want to lord it over anyone. I'm more of a facilitator, one who walks alongside people and empowers them to build their own identities. A position like Lord of the World just doesn't feel right to me.*

Or perhaps orthodoxy is the missing ingredient here.

*Look, I would take the deal, Lucifer, but the Father and I have this plan for me to die, and I need people to believe that my death has a sacrificial effect that connects them to God. Taking control of all the kingdoms of the world might make things too good for humankind, and they might not come to terms with their need for a personal savior.*

No, you're right. Literally no one can imagine any of these scenarios, whatever moralistic, theological, or political use they make of the passage. Neither titles and luxury nor the longing for human approval could tempt a man already enthroned as King of Kings and Lord of Lords, and Satan knew very well with whom he was dealing. Yet in Matthew's account, this temptation is saved for last, and one senses it may have been the worst of the three. What about this offer did Satan think would be so enticing for Jesus?

Imagine with me what doing obeisance before Satan would allow Jesus to accomplish. He could institute utopia on earth, the best relative justice available to imperfect, unjust human beings. It would mean a qualitatively different future for the world. Imagine the lives saved, the bestial inhumanity people perpetrate on each other stopped forever. Imagine the end of war, poverty, and oppression.

If Jesus didn't accept, however, it meant letting the world go its way. He would then need to call men and women out of the world who wished to follow him, creating a different kind of community than the world had seen before: the church. Jesus knew where this path would lead. Rejecting Satan's offer put him on the road to humiliation, torture, and a violent death. The same would be true of anyone who accepted his kingdom as the rightful one. That is why Jesus said in John's Gospel, "If you belonged to the world, it would love you as its own. As it is, you do not belong to the world, but I have chosen you out of the world" (15:19). It was into this sort of story that Jesus was calling his followers.

What then could possibly be said in favor of *rejecting* Satan's offer? The American public theologian Reinhold Niebuhr and his intellectual descendants on both right and left would find Jesus's actions unpardonably irresponsible. In taking this route, he chose pain and ruin for both the world and himself. Only a foolish and selfish obsession with principles or a fanatical need to keep our hands clean would motivate most of us to let such a deal go.

But Jesus sees what we cannot. He understood and understands the depravity of the human heart. The reality is that even the best of us could not live in the utopia Satan offered.

This should have been clear all along since the kingdoms of relative justice so many give their lives for today are *always* established and maintained on a foundation of oppression. The human heart is twisted and torn from many lifetimes of resentment and covetousness, generations in which assault and withdrawal form patterns of interpersonal communication, and our genetic codes bend over millennia toward sin. We cannot build or live in a truly Christian nation because *we human beings are still unjust*. Yes, there are yet tares among the wheat and goats among the sheep, but the wheat itself is still part tare and the sheep still part goat. Even if somehow in the blink of an eye Christ made all of our broken social structures truly just, but without making *us truly* just, the world would still be one of pain and brokenness beyond reckoning. To heal these ancient and enduring wounds, Jesus cannot just take on structural and social injustices, the principalities and powers of this dark world. He also had to show *us* how to live the kingdom's politics. He must train us for a new way of life.

A truly Christian nation is impossible for the same reason such a utopia of relative justice is impossible—because sinful human beings govern Christian nations too. A Christian nation cannot bring the kingdom of God. A government cannot, in other words, exist in the world as it is *and also* live the gospel. Everyone knows this, of course, even Niebuhr and Stephen Wolfe and those in their respective camps. They just believe the word *Christian* should be deployed *apart from* the gospel in service of a (supposedly) desirable relative justice. But that way leads to the name of Christ being tarnished and the political meaning of the gospel being forgotten—both of which have happened among us.

Jesus took a different path. And here we must pay attention, for in chapters four and five of his gospel, Matthew brings the nature of Christian political life into view. Immediately after returning from his ordeal in the desert, Jesus began his ministry. "From that time Jesus began to proclaim, 'Repent, for the kingdom of heaven has come near'" (Matt. 4:17). Repent (*metanoia*), as I said earlier, literally means "change your mind." Notice that, according to Jesus, the reason why we should change our mind is that *a different political reality is on the horizon*. It's not here yet in its fullness. But Jesus announces its coming to any who will listen.

Most messiahs at this point would have been eyeballs deep in military planning. They thought the new political reality God was bringing about was a free Israel, a nation delivered from foreign occupiers. In Jesus's time the Roman superpower had the Jews under their thumb, and if this were the moment God had chosen to set them free, they had to be ready to play their part. Judas the Galilean had done so when Jesus was about ten years old, and some credit him with sparking the Zealot movement, a theocratic anti-tax and anti-census movement to counter Roman power. The horrific Jewish War (AD 66–70), which ended with the destruction of Jerusalem and the temple, and Simon bar Kokhba's rebellion (AD 132–135) were fueled by the same hopes.

We do not, by contrast, find Jesus stockpiling arms to protect his family from the Roman government or consciously making friends in high places to maintain his religious freedom. Instead, at the very outset of his ministry, we find him *founding a community* (4:18). He called this community to leave behind key relationships, property, and security. When they joined Jesus's community, they necessarily also committed themselves to a life of poverty. He hung out in Galilee, preaching to growing crowds instead of going up to Jerusalem, as any up-and-coming politico in Israel knew he should. The wrong people seemed to congregate around him, which meant he was constantly sending the wrong signals to the political establishment, and he actively encouraged such losers. The first men he called to join his community, Peter and Andrew, were from what we can tell entirely unknown. Worse, Peter repeatedly misunderstood Jesus's intentions at critical moments. Jesus also took into his inner circle Matthew, a tax collector whom many Israelites would therefore have seen as a traitor, and Simon, a Zealot whose political ideology called for terrorism and reprisals against people like Matthew. As any consulting firm working with would-be messiahs could have told him, this was not best practice.

But Jesus was not *other* messiahs. After Jesus's introduction to public life, Matthew immediately gives us his most famous sermon, a sermon that, likely as not, was the sort of thing Jesus preached all the time. In it he sets out to describe the politics of his new community. Here the poor in spirit, the pure in heart, and peacemakers become institutional pillars, not necessarily the inspiring, educated, administratively gifted, or ambitious. The community holds out a vision of the future in which, of all people, the meek will inherit the earth and those persecuted now for the sake of righteousness will find themselves on top. Some of those who are last now will then be first, and, indeed, some of those first now will be last. So the community Jesus founded looks forward to the day when that change comes—the day the Bible calls "the day of the Lord"—by hungering and thirsting for righteousness in public and within themselves. Jesus assures them that that passionate desire, despite the way things look now, will one day be sated.

In the meantime, Jesus's followers are not just to refrain from murder and assault, but also to reject anger and insults; not just stay faithful to their spouses or celibacy commitments, but to shun lust; not only to foreswear revenge, but, in doing so, to risk being taken advantage of; not simply to take care of their families and be good neighbors, but to do good and wish good upon those who hate them. They are not even to worry about their own futures, but rather to invest everything they have in Jesus's reign and the community whose political existence gives us a foretaste of what that reign will be like.

Dear reader, Jesus has a *politics called the church*, and you are invited to take part in it. It is revolutionary, but not at all in the usual sense of that word. It is humanist, but only if you mean a humanism that roots the inestimable worth of human beings in God. It is neither liberal nor conservative. Or, just maybe, it is both of them at once. Perhaps it goes without saying that we cannot transplant these politics into DC culture. We cannot, in fact, transplant them into any national culture that has ever existed among humans.

Which is why Jesus founded a community and not a nation. Nation-states must control territory to stay in existence. They therefore police that territory and defend its borders by maintaining a monopoly on violence. They stockpile weapons that could destroy the planet many times over for fear of what their enemies might do if they let down their guard.

Jesus's community, by contrast, controlled no territory because, given the sinful world we live in, their politics of enemy love, peaceableness, meekness, and the like made that impossible. Some might respond that human beings need space in the world to carry on their political life. Without land, buildings, and places that they can claim as their own, doing politics becomes impossible. That's undoubtedly true. But Jesus's community does have such space. In one sense, they claim the whole world. They trust that their Lord will one day say "no more" to injustice, sin, hatred, and death and wipe away every tear from their eyes. Then their politics will be the way the world actually works. In the interim, however, Jesus's community has only one space in this world to practice their way of life together: under the cross of Christ.

They are, after all, following Christ in trying to live a fully human politics in an inhumane world. As the Catholic theologian Herbert McCabe put it,

> Jesus did nothing but be the Son as man; that his life was so colourful, eventful and tragic is simply because of what being human involves in *our* world. We for the most part shy off being human because if we are really human we will be crucified. If we didn't know that before, we know it now; the crucifixion of Jesus was simply the dramatic manifestation of the sort of world we have made, the showing up of the world, the unmasking of what we call, traditionally, original sin. There is no need whatever for peculiar theories about the Father deliberately putting his Son to death. There is no need for *any* theory about the death of Jesus. It doesn't need any explanation once you know that he was human in *our* world. Jesus died in obedience to the Father's will simply in the sense that he was *human* in obedience to the Father's will.[1]

The inevitable result of the church's politics in our world is that in infinitely varied ways Christians will reflect their Lord by becoming like him in his death; thus we also, in infinitely varied ways, find ourselves in Gethsemane on the way to Calvary. As is true of his death on the tree, Jesus's agonized prayer, his fear, his isolation, and his decision to trust his Father also become the story of his body, the church. And that should hardly surprise us. This is the sort of thing that tends to happen to resident aliens in our world. Peter, Diognetus's Christian friend, and others in the early church knew it. More importantly, Jesus knew it. He knew that the inhumane politics of our world would never let him escape alive. Yet when that terrible and decisive moment came, he did not choose the world's politics, but lived to the limit the politics he himself had preached. "Put your sword back in its place . . . for all who draw the sword will die by the sword. Do you think I cannot call on my Father, and he will at once put at my disposal more than twelve legions of angels?" (Matt. 26:52–53). He lived a politics that simply did not and does not work in this broken world—but it's the *only* politics that will work in the world of the new creation.

Which, if we think about it, means that the political abasement the church must experience now will not be eternal. As the Father vindicated the Son's political life in the resurrection, so God will vindicate the politics of the church in the Day of the Lord when many of those who have been last and least—those who have embodied the politics of meekness even as they thirsted for true justice—will suddenly, to the astonishment of everyone, be first. "Do you not know that we will judge angels?" Paul asked the Corinthians (1 Cor. 6:3), and he did not mean this as a figure of speech. In his second letter to the Corinthians, he encouraged them not to lose heart, saying that "inwardly we are being renewed day by day" because "our light and momentary troubles are achieving for us an eternal glory" (2 Cor. 4:16).

Paul was clear-headed in this hope. So were the other New Testament writers. In 2 Timothy 2:12, we're told that "if we endure, we will also reign with him," and 2 Peter speaks of a new heavens and a new earth where, as I translate it, "justice is home" (3:13). In Revelation we find that all those who endure in living this politics become part of the city of God, the first truly just and the first truly humane society, the political community of a redeemed and renewed people. Jesus's rejection of Satan's offer on the mountain and the church's renunciation of violence, manipulation, and hatred of enemies make sense if and only if we have this hope.

In the here and now, however, few will believe in our eventual vindication for living this way. What they'll see when we reject faith in money, manipulation, and Machiavellianism is foolishness and failure—and major organizations rarely list the foolishness of God among their core values. So be it. Our job is to point to the politics of the future—the kingdom of God—by the way we live now in our own church communities.

So then, you ask, what does this concretely mean? Do we take up political quietism, stop voting, be tax resisters? Not necessarily—though in some situations any and all of these might be necessary. Primarily the gospel enjoins us to positive action, not just to adopt a litany of antis. Love your neighbor, go the second mile, bind up the wounds of those caught in the wheels of the political-economic machine, feed the hungry, welcome the immigrant, stand with the oppressed, be present with the forgotten and lonely, encourage the church, and preach the gospel! We all already know that we should be doing these things.

At times, however, speaking antis is the only way to speak in concert with the gospel. At times we must simply say no and say it loud and clear. Certain political situations in our world will inevitably leave us in what Protestants traditionally called a *status confessionis*, a Latin term meaning roughly a situation in which our confession of Christ's lordship is at stake and we must speak or act accordingly. Failing to do so amounts to a denial of the gospel.

Potential examples of such situations are easy to come by. Dietrich Bonhoeffer spoke of the German church being in a *status confessionis* after Hitler came to power and antisemitic legislation was applied to the church.[2] Today some might argue that liberal abortion laws put the church in a *status confessionis*, though arguments about post-*Roe* American political realities as well as arguments about early term fetal life do complicate that case. Severely restrictionist immigration policies also might leave the church in a *status confessionis*, but just what sort of laws or international humanitarian crises might trigger it is difficult to say beforehand.

So what would constitute a *status confessionis* then? We might talk about it in several ways, but traditionally Protestant thinkers used the term for political situations like the following:

1. The government interferes in the life of the church by forbidding preaching or discussion about the gospel or any implication of the gospel.
2. The government uses the form of the gospel or the church's prestige in society to forward a gospel-distorting agenda.

3.   A political reality puts serious barriers in the way of preaching the gospel.

Notice that revoking the church's tax-exempt status is not a *status confessionis*. The legalization of gay marriage is not a *status confessionis*. Neither is the popularization in certain urban areas of "drag queen story hour" or local schools including LGBTQ materials in their curricula. Such things happen in the world. That should hardly surprise us. The critical consideration is that they do not warp the message of the kingdom. Our job is not to make the world into the church. It is to call people out of the world through the proclamation of the gospel message, and in particular calling Americans out of the darkness of national politics as usual and into the wondrous light of the politics of the church. Many act as if putting a stop to "drag queen story hour" identifies what Christianity is and does, but often enough that just baptizes a traditionalist American culture. In doing so, we actually point others toward "another gospel" that is diametrically opposed to the gospel of the Crucified. In addition to explicit narration of the Jesus story, proclamation of the true gospel, by contrast, might involve serving trans people in practical ways despite or, indeed, because of our concerns for their long-term well-being.

Even religious-liberty issues should almost never get the label of *status confessionis*. That is because rights have nothing whatsoever to do with our politics as Christians. No one should think the relitigation of the *Masterpiece Cakeshop* Supreme Court case, for example, shows that the church must stand up for its confession. If a baker has to stop baking wedding cakes or only make preset designs to avoid baking a cake for a gay wedding, that is not a *status confessionis*. We might feel sorry for this brother or sister in Christ; it might be a major inconvenience or worse, and the church might do well to help him or her in any number of ways. But there is simply no theological—that is, *gospel-shaped*—path to the claim that the church's confession is at stake here. Instead, a Christian should change his or her business. Stop doing specialized wedding cakes outside of certain preset designs. Quit altogether if it becomes necessary, as difficult as that is. Refuse to make your life about protecting your own interests and instead make it about serving your neighbors, including your LGBTQ neighbors, particularly those who are brothers and sisters in the faith (even if we believe they've missed the mark).

In short, live the politics of the gospel, and reject the gospel of America. Only when (1) the former is forbidden or (2) the latter is demanded do you have a *status confessionis*.

Democratic governments in today's world have rarely made demands like these on the church. The danger nowadays usually comes in the form of the third type of situation I listed above, when a political situation throws up a barrier in the way of gospel proclamation. Frequently enough, such political situations *invite and encourage* a misapplication or misunderstanding of the gospel.

The American church faces just such a *status confessionis* in the presidential candidacy of Donald Trump. By that, I mean straightforwardly that *because we are Christians we must not* vote for this man, and *we must* speak against his perversions of the gospel and corruption of the life of the church. That does not mean it is our job to keep Trump from a second term in the White House. It does not mean that the republic will collapse if Trump wins nor even necessarily that a Trump presidency will, by some yardsticks, be worse than a Biden presidency. None of these things should be our primary concern. Our primary concern should be that by voting for and publicly supporting Donald Trump, Christians distort the gospel and erect a barrier to hearing that message that for many people none but God can surmount.

Most of us long ago had our fill of Trump and Trumpian controversy. Since 2015 friendships have dissolved, resentment and mistrust surfaced, and churches divided because of this man. Rehashing old debates about him no doubt sounds exhausting and unfruitful. But we must.

We must because more than any American political figure in recent memory, Donald Trump and the political realities he has created have perverted the gospel that is the life of the church. More than even his policies, he has done this through his rhetoric, his promises, and what he has told the church to fear. We must examine that rhetoric and those promises, both those given explicitly and those put forward implicitly, and in so doing uncover the source of the roiling fear that today threatens to choke the life of the Spirit among us.

# 6

# TRUMP AND
# THE GOSPEL OF AMERICA

"This is the final battle," Trump's disembodied voice says.

The scene is a nondescript hallway in an upscale build-ing. Everything is in black and white, and an anxious, percussive musical score rises in the background. A moment later, the camera shifts slightly and the former president himself comes into view, advancing down a long hallway, his mouth taut and a quiet rage in his eyes. As he walks, the voice-over continues: "With you at my side, we will demolish the deep state, we will expel the warmongers from our government, we will drive out the globalists, we will cast out the communists, Marxists, and fascists. We will throw off the sick political class that hates our country. We will rout the fake news media, and we will liberate America from these villains once and for all."[1]

Trump posted this campaign ad to his Truth Social account on July 2, 2023. Few noticed it, perhaps because this is the sort of thing Trump says all the time or because nowadays violent political rhetoric seems, relatively speaking, inbounds. We, however, should take note. This chilling thirty-second clip represents something new in American politics: a professionally produced ad approved by the Republican frontrunner for president that could easily be interpreted as a call to arms. It constitutes a thinly veiled threat to American democracy.

But the Trump movement threatens something more important than democracy. It threatens the gospel of Jesus Christ and therefore the very life of the church in America. While you and I may find ourselves grateful for much of what America has heretofore offered and work together to preserve that way of life, the church has existed and, indeed, thrived under many forms of government, not just democratic ones. It could survive and perhaps even thrive after the collapse of democracy. Further, averting the collapse of the American political system is not really the business of the church. The proclamation of the gospel and living out that gospel in public is.

One day, likely as not, American democracy will go the way of all the earth. The church, however, will remain. Jesus told us as much: "Heaven and earth will pass away, but my words will never pass away" (Matt. 24:37). But for a variety of reasons the church can and has withered in certain corners of the world, and the rise of Donald Trump brings with it the grim prospect that this could happen in America too. We could hardly blame it on persecution. Instead, the gospel evangelicals actually believe has given them less and less reason to be a part of the church.

As we have seen, this is because, like culture warriors before him, Trump's rhetoric and actions implicitly ask Christians to believe in another, American gospel. The Trump movement is not evangelicalism's best hope to wrest religious freedom from the grasp of a purportedly totalitarian liberalism. It represents the loss of the only religious freedom that matters: the proclamation of the gospel. Trumpism is the colonization of the church by the nation, a colonization carried out in public even as it is repeatedly and forcefully denied.

Think of how American products, mores, and modes of commerce entered underdeveloped nations. Once certain ideas, practices, and technologies had a foothold, it was only a matter of time before the local populace found their old ways of life impossible to maintain. Trumpism has colonized evangelical life in similarly surreptitious ways. Living the way of Christ in churches where the fruit of the Spirit is part of our political life together becomes harder and harder when Trumpism or Trump-strategy thinking provides the background assumptions about how the Christian life actually works. The Moral Majority, Fundamentalism, and perhaps establishment Protestant liberalism paved the way for this colonization. With Trumpism, however, full colonization is underway.

Subtle differences between traditional American civil religion and Trumpism may be making this pill easier to swallow for some evangelicals. In America, public rhetoric about religious matters has always had a place for the Bible, but politicians almost never make use of the name of Jesus Christ. Days that honor members of the armed forces who shed their blood for us—that is, make "the ultimate sacrifice"—perhaps provide a faint, distorted echo of Christ's work on the cross. But American civil religion has no place for Jesus himself. It is instead, as Robert Bellah saw so clearly, vaguely Unitarian and, above all, providentially involved with American democracy and its exceptional greatness.[2] The Fourth of July and Memorial Day are among its high holy days, but they're not days of repentance. Perfunctory expressions of regret over slavery and Jim Crow racism are fine, but nothing that might threaten America's exceptional mission to the world.

Most of this civil religion remains popular among Trump supporters, and, when need be, Trump himself deploys its core ideas with at least passable facility. Remember Trump's infamous Bible-in-hand photo op at St. John's church in Washington? This was hardly a unique moment. Bill Clinton and other presidents were also photographed toting their Bibles outside churches. Like presidents before him, Trump quoted Scripture in his first inaugural address in order to bring Americans of every faith together under the flag. He lauds the armed forces, venerates past American greats like Andrew Jackson and Teddy Roosevelt, and attacks those whose interest in racial justice seems to threaten American exceptionalism—all of which, by itself, hardly makes him unique.[3] One might even conceivably see the motivation for Trump's America First stance as making America a city on a hill "again."

Yet Trump is different for a key reason. Among adherents of the civil religion arising from the American gospel, Trump has altered doctrine at one key *locus*. A "Christological" component has been added that both subtly alters its theology, increases its power, and affects other *loci* in critical ways. This Christological component, of course, is Trump himself.

To grasp the significance of this change, let's look at the other doctrines first, starting with eschatology. Think about the effect of the former president's constant claims that the "final battle" with evil liberals has now commenced. What does this claim *do*? It quite clearly provides the other, American gospel with an eschatology that echoes traditional evangelical readings of Revelation, one that makes it look more "Christian." While Trumpism is surely incapable of producing anything with the grandeur and gravitas of John's apocalypse, here too we have the hope of a new polity in which evil is finally defeated (or rather viciously avenged) and the righteous are vindicated. Here Trump himself, of course, stands in the place of the Revelation's triumphant Christ, and the extraordinary promises Trump makes depend upon him possessing such power.

The doctrine of atonement too gets warped because of Trump's Christological move. In a Truth Social post on August 3, 2023, Trump wrote:

I AM NOW GOING TO WASHINGTON, D.C., TO BE ARRESTED FOR HAVING CHALLENGED A CORRUPT, RIGGED, & STOLEN ELECTION. IT IS A GREAT HONOR, BECAUSE I AM BEING ARRESTED FOR YOU. MAKE AMERICA GREAT AGAIN!!![4]

The former president struck the same notes after his first indictment in New York. "They want to silence me because I will never let them silence you," Trump said at an April 2023 event. "They want you silenced. And I'm the only one who can save this nation because you know that they're not coming after me, they're coming after you, and I just happen to be standing in the way. And I will never be moving."[5]

Notice the substitutionary rhetoric. Notice the claims—both of which are almost constantly on his lips—that he is "the only one who can save this nation" and that "they're coming after you," but he stands in the way. Like in Russia, liberals ("they") take on the role of Satan (which allows extreme measures to be taken against them), while Trump is unjustly persecuted *in the place of his followers*. "It's kind of a Jesus Christ thing," a source close to Trump's legal team told *Vanity Fair*. "He is saying, 'I'm absorbing all this pain from all around from everywhere so you don't have to' [and] 'If they can do this to me, they can do this to you' . . . that's a powerful message."[6]

That pain—the resentment, obsession, and fear of Trump's base—has given birth to a perverted ecclesiology, a purportedly "Christian" community that shuns the politics of the church. When Trump, numerous aides, and lawyers were arrested in the Georgia state election-interference case, attorney Jenna Ellis tweeted a picture of her mugshot. Despite being charged with wire fraud, she was grinning ear to ear, obviously quite pleased with herself. The text above her picture read, "But I say unto you, love your enemies, bless them that curse you, do good to them that hate you, and pray for them that despitefully use you and persecute you."[7]

What did Ellis mean? Not necessarily that one should do good to liberals, though, to her credit, her timeline is largely free of the venomous tone and slanderous claims typical of the Christian-nationalist set. Neither did she mean that Trump was the best man for the job in 2024. Until Ron DeSantis dropped his bid for the presidency in January, she was clear he would have her vote.[8] Instead, by pairing her now-famous Fulton County jail photo with Jesus's famous admonition, Ellis meant to communicate several things at once. (1) Conservatives are Jesus's people, (2) conservatives like her are being persecuted, and (3) liberals are their persecutors. (4) Therefore, conservatives are righteous and (5) liberals are unrighteous. Consequently, they cannot be Jesus's people.

Notice what has happened: Ellis's gospel is manifestly about America rather than about Jesus Christ, and Jesus has been enlisted in her struggle to realize her conservative vision of America. Which side of the aisle gets to call itself righteous is hardly my point. Look instead at Ellis's ecclesiology: the church has been completely supplanted by the nation. Probably without thinking about it, evangelicals like Ellis have substituted the church's politics (and, for that matter, ethics) for the politics and ethical code of the nation.

This substitution shows up in what Trump says about his base. In a much-watched interview with Tucker Carlson on the night of the first Republican primary debate, Trump lauded the character of those who took part in the insurrection on January 6, 2021. "There's tremendous passion and there's tremendous love. . . . People who were in that crowd that day . . . said it was the most beautiful day they'd ever experienced. There was love in that crowd—there was love and unity. I have never seen such passion, such spirit, and such love . . . and simultaneously such hatred."[9]

But what spirit did he mean? Which unity and what love? Surely not the *Holy* Spirit, the fruits of which are love, joy, peace, patience, kindness, goodness, faithfulness, gentleness, and self-control. Clearly this unity was not one of that Spirit, the Spirit which calls *the church* together. Obviously, this love it not the sort of love that "is not self-seeking" (1 Cor. 13:5).

On the contrary, this is an altogether different sort of spirit. Violent rhetoric and, as Trump himself recognized, hatred are its fruit. Doesn't this crowd's behavior and the behavior of its leaders bear a stronger resemblance to Paul's list describing the sinful nature: "sexual immorality, impurity, and debauchery . . . hatred, discord, jealousy, fits of rage, selfish ambition, dissensions, factions, and envy" (Gal. 5:19–21)? Is the unity Trump spoke about not born of shared resentment? Is the love he witnessed the sort which might love its enemies as Jesus taught us—or is it rather closer to killing them?

We could hardly ask for a better demonstration of how Christian nationalists warp Christian life and doctrine. The eschatology, atonement, ecclesiology, and ethics these evangelicals actually live bear no real resemblance to traditional Christian doctrine. One just has to have eyes to see and ears to hear what they (or, rather, we) actually say and do.

Now we must address the reason for these changes in America's gospel and the driving force behind evangelicalism's deepening embrace of Christian-nationalist heresy: Trump's gauche portrayal of himself as a kind of messiah. For the first few years of his presidency, not a few evangelicals compared the famous reality television star to King Cyrus, and their point was not just that Cyrus was a pagan king who was friendly toward God's people and used the power of his empire for their good.[10] Isaiah 45:1 calls Cyrus an "anointed one"—that is, a messiah. Even then, some evangelicals believed God had placed Trump in an almost messianic role.

He certainly didn't mind. On August 24, 2019, reporters from CNN and other networks assailed him outside the White House with questions about the escalating trade war with China. The president, leaning toward his interlocutors and gesticulating with characteristic intensity, had come in for criticism for insulting and provoking the Chinese, and journalists could safely bet his reaction would be newsworthy.

"Somebody said it's Trump's trade war. This isn't my trade war. This is a trade war that should have taken place a long time ago by a lot of other presidents," he said. "Somebody had to do it."

Then glancing up at the sky with mock solemnity, Trump said, "I am the chosen one."[11]

A harmless joke, some might say, and by itself they would surely be right. But widen your lens a bit. Take in the whole Trump-political saga from his ride down the escalator at Trump Tower when he announced his 2015 presidential campaign to the January 6, 2021, Capitol insurrection to the 2024 Republican primary. Remember the frequency with which the real estate mogul has said, "I am the only one who can save America," a phrase Susan B. Glasser has called the "messianic signature" of his 2024 campaign.[12] Notice how often he makes claims that would require near omnipotence (for example, that he could end the Russia-Ukraine war in a day). What comes into focus is that on some level Trump actually believes his own messianic rhetoric. And so do very many evangelicals.[13]

This is the core reason why the American church is currently in a *status confessionis* regarding Trump support. To put the matter as simply as possible, a Christian cannot support Donald Trump's bid for the presidency. Our confession of Christ as Lord demands that we say no to the Trump movement and refuse to vote for him. After all, one simply cannot live both Trump's politics and the politics of the church. We have to choose.

What happens if American evangelicals choose wrongly? Some will think it wise to resist the urge to ask questions like this. Like the sensationalist preacher telling his audience to mark their calendars for the second coming, prognosticators are usually most persuasive before the evidence for their claims comes in. Questions like this one can, in other words, be used to manipulate one's audience.

But, as Jesus said, "wisdom is proved right by her deeds" (Matt. 11:19). And, we should add, so also is folly proved wrong. The historical and contemporary examples we have considered give us more than enough reason to say that Christian nationalism and its cousin, culture-war evangelicalism, miss the logic of the gospel. For that reason, while the world's wisdom justifies these approaches after a fashion, the light of the gospel reveals them for the utter foolishness that they are. They have long been the source of the rot in contemporary evangelicalism. "Looking at it now," Russell Moore said in a recent interview, "we can see that there were patterns in place all along that many of us didn't recognize at the time leading to this place."[14] He who has ears, let him hear.

We evangelicals have placed more importance upon religious freedom than on the proclamation and performance of the gospel. We have obsessed about the good that power can do and considered irrelevant the good that God is doing. We have fretted about self-preservation in ways that are the very definition of faithlessness. These are the tracks on which the Trump train runs, and, at the very least, they extend some ways back into American history. If we stay on this track, we can know with fair certainty where it leads.

First, evangelical churches will secularize or, rather, continue to secularize until churches are a fraction of the size they are now. That doesn't necessarily mean that the surrounding culture's secularization will put pressure on evangelicals until they decide to leave the church, though that could happen too. It means that, absent a renewed hearing and doing of the word, the gospel story will get further and further from the center of whatever common life is left in evangelical congregations. The felt identity of an evangelical congregation will continue to warp, bending ever more decisively toward their vision of American life instead of the gospel-oriented life of the church community. In other words, unless something changes, we will see churches ever more firmly embrace the gospel of America—and thereby abandon the hope of the true gospel.

Both anecdotal evidence and hard data tell us that this is already happening. Former Trump National Security Advisor Michael Flynn provides an astonishing example of the former in a talk he gave at a church last year. "There is an effort by dark forces . . . to rewrite the Bible," he told congregants. "And they're going to do it using AI!"[15] In the same talk, however, he told pastors to "put the Bible aside and read the Constitution during some of your sermons," launching into a passionate paean to America's Founding Fathers. If the irony occurred to him, it didn't show, and he awkwardly wrapped up that part of the talk by forcefully assuring those present that the Founders' writings were "based primarily on the Bible."[16]

Flynn fits right into parts of the evangelical mainstream. Few may buy his first take, but most readers will know a friend or relative who, like Flynn, feels Christianity is under attack in America. Though many might blanch at putting the Bible aside in church, Flynn's claim that American government is biblically based is simply assumed by the majority of evangelicals—though almost no one attempts to support that belief with Scripture or historical evidence. Flynn and evangelicals like him then put those two beliefs together and get two more: that an assault on the Bible is also an assault on America and vice versa, and we are responsible for stopping both.

In this way evangelicals have fallen from faith in the gospel of Jesus Christ and gravitated toward the gospel of America. In Flynn's claims above, we can see secularization happening inside the church.

The data tells us that this ecclesial secularization has happened simultaneously with the greatest decline in church attendance in modern American history. Early in the pandemic the Barna Group reported that a third of practicing Christians had stopped attending church.[17] More than half never returned.[18] It turns out, however, that the pandemic only exacerbated a larger trend. The average US congregation in 2020 was half the size it had been in 2000.[19] The slow exit of Americans from religious institutions which has gone on since the early 1970s has become a dash for the doors—and, most striking of all, in recent years conservative Americans are by far the most likely to leave.[20]

This last data point will surprise many people. LGBTQ issues, politics, and careerism are the common reasons people cite to explain the great American de-churching, and, to be sure, these are part of the picture.[21] But to stop there means overlooking the epicenter of the problem.

Which brings us to another likely outcome of evangelicals choosing the gospel of America: at least for a while, they will continue to claim the mantle of evangelicalism. In a fascinating article in *Christianity Today*, historian Daniel K. Williams used General Social Survey data to show just how many self-described Southern evangelicals have quit church. "If 'lapsed evangelical Protestant' were a denomination," Williams writes, "it would be by far the largest religious body in the South."[22] Williams found that these former churchgoers don't become liberals when they stop going to church. Their views on marijuana and sex loosen up somewhat, but their general political outlook remains the same. They continue to oppose abortion, and more than half still think removing prayer from public schools was a mistake. Most astonishing of all, 89 percent of these lapsed Southern evangelicals continue to believe the Bible is the word of God; a third say it must be "taken literally, word for word."

What could make someone who believes that the Bible is to be "taken literally, word for word" stop going to church? Perhaps they have always said they believed such things, and putting it down on an anonymous survey meant little to them. Or because some corners of Southern and Midwestern culture reward such statements, they checked that box automatically even on an anonymous survey. Or maybe they want to be the sort of person who believes the Bible is the word of God, but actually, if pushed to think about it, they really don't.

All of these hypotheses make sense to a degree. But there's a cleaner explanation that accounts for the data: *going to church just isn't religiously necessary for many evangelicals.* They aren't lying when they call themselves evangelical and tell pollsters what they believe. They may experience a little cognitive dissonance now and again—an evangelical talking head hints that living together before marriage isn't great or they hear someone mention that passage about "loving the foreigner as yourself" and have a fleeting thought about the anti-immigration policies they vociferously support. But on the whole, they feel that they're regular, Bible-believing evangelical Christians who do the best they can.

But the best they can—when performed under their own power and not in the power of the Spirit—is not living the gospel of Jesus Christ. That gospel is meant to be lived out in the church community. Instead, many of these evangelicals have latched onto another, different gospel, the gospel of America, which is lived out within the community of the nation-state. "It seems," Williams writes, "that when white Southerners stop attending church, they don't lose the church's political conservatism, moralism, or individualism. Instead, they become hyper-individualistic, strongly devoted to law and order, and overwhelmingly politically conservative (if they vote at all). But they're also cynical and distrustful of others."

This cynicism arises in part because the community they identify with—for example, Southern rural conservatives—is bound together by different memories than those of the church. The church is bound together, first of all, by the grand narrative found in the Scriptures from which, by the power of the Spirit, the gospel comes to us today. Secondarily, what God has done in our local church community in the past provides us with our sense of identity. Those who see themselves as first Southern or Midwestern conservatives—or "real Americans" of whatever stripe—will have other collective memories that connect them with their community. These may be memories of a valuable heritage (1776) or triumph (World War II), but today they are perhaps more likely to be memories of collectively felt injury (the Lost Cause, *Brown v. Board*, restrictions of prayer in school, Barack Obama's election, the *Obergefell* case that legalized gay marriage, wokeness, or the investigation into Trump's ties with Russia). Or perhaps for many, that collectively felt injury arose less from any one lost political battle than from a generalized feeling that their people had been disrespected—say, with the loss of representation in mainstream national media and higher education that has unfolded over the past two generations. Either way, the collective memories that bind these Christian nationalists, culture-war evangelicals, or "real Americans" together have bred a festering and, indeed, addictive resentment.

These memories and the resentment that arises from them may be food and drink for today's conservatives, but both are poison for the church community. The church orients its common life around different memories and around different hopes. The problem is that Christian nationalism and the true gospel are found within the same churches, and, as Russell Moore noted, many couldn't see what was happening until recent crises forced the division into the light.

Both Christian nationalists and the gospel evangelicals speak of the Bible as the word of God. But for one, it's a coffee-table decoration, a part of their Sunday attire—or, better, a totem. For the other, the stories in it tell them what God has done for humanity in the past, who God is shown to be in Christ—and, therefore, who they are. Both many Christian nationalists and many gospel evangelicals oppose gay marriage. But Christian nationalists see the *Obergefell* case that legalized gay marriage nationally as a threat to their power and a threat to the church. By contrast, gospel evangelicals, whatever their sexual orientation, see it as an opportunity to live in faith and obedience to the gospel in public. Even as they accompany their gay brothers and sisters on their journeys and urge them to continue in celibacy, they rejoice that *Obergefell* has lessened the intolerable and reprehensible burdens borne for so long by so many. Both Christian nationalists and gospel evangelicals are concerned about their neighbors.

Christian nationalists often fear them: that they will take away their "God-given" freedoms, speak ill of them, and induce their children to rebel against them. Gospel evangelicals love not just their neighbors, but their enemies, pray for the neighbor who thinks them immoral, and, when they fail to do these things, they ask for forgiveness and help from God and their church community. These divisions cannot be papered over with nice-sounding words, institutional cheerleading, or sticking our heads in the sand. They are fundamental.

For that reason, to the degree that evangelicals choose the gospel of America over the gospel of Jesus Christ, churches will splinter. Many who now call themselves evangelical will then be hardened toward the gospel. Some may well be people we love. Nevertheless, there will be a remnant. The biblical story should lead us to believe this much—not because of our rightness or because that's the way the world works, but because of who God is.

Jesus's ministry began with his descent from the mountain where he refused the devil's means of saving the world. His ministry drew to a close as he approached another mountain, the Temple Mount at the center of Jerusalem. There he would be murdered under the direction of the religious authorities. Talking about tearing down the temple and raising it again in three days just sounded too much like a threat to the people's nationalist religious identity. Forcing Jerusalemites to reckon with how far temple economics had deviated from the Torah's prescription was a bridge too far. Jerusalem would reject him and his politics, and he knew it.

Weeping publicly, Jesus spoke to those traveling with him about the city's near future, a future that arrived during the Jewish War thirty-five years later. Armies would encircle Jerusalem. People would starve. Children would be killed. The city walls and the temple itself would be torn down, and not one stone would be left upon another. "If you, even you, had only known on this day what would bring you peace," Jesus said, looking up at the city, "but now it is hidden from your eyes" (Luke 19:41-42).

As a movement, evangelicalism has lost the way of peace. It has been hidden from our eyes, and it seems we're unlikely to find it again without a reckoning—what used to be called judgment. My point in this book has not been that evangelicals have been treated just fine in being forced to the periphery of American culture over the last generation. It's that we never should have made it our business to fight for a seat at the nation's table. In the process, we abandoned our stated reason for maintaining a foothold in government, universities, and creative industries in the first place, which is to season their institutional cultures with the salt of the gospel. Instead, we have taken hold of another, distinctly American gospel that ultimately cannot coexist with the true gospel, a gospel that has turned American culture insipid rather than preserving it for the kingdom. There are only two paths out of this spiritual cul-de-sac: repentance or judgment.

As Germans slowly began the business of rebuilding their lives after the Second World War, a saying became current in the southwestern city of Mannheim: "*Erst mal wieder Grund reinbringen*" or "First get a piece of land."[23] You probably feel something of that sentiment yourself: Plan, work hard, pursue your goals, and, no matter how bad things look now, one day you'll enjoy their fruit. But in the shock of losing everything, even the basic infrastructure that makes modern lives possible, few Mannheimers asked themselves how it had all happened. The Holocaust, the colonialist war of extermination in Eastern Europe, what the displaced foreigners who wandered their streets endured—none of that concerned them. The acid taste of resentment and the terrible fragility of their futures were what mattered to them. In that they were no different than most other Germans.

If judgment comes upon the American evangelical movement, our first move when it is over cannot be "first get a piece of land." It cannot be to ask, How quickly and efficiently can we rebuild to make a life and a future for ourselves? Instead, those of us who remain should let ourselves appear to other Americans like what we are: foreigners whose citizenship is in another kingdom, resident aliens for whom the institutions we build and the homes we make must be held with an open hand. To quote Dietrich Bonhoeffer, we "take the next necessary step" to further God's kingdom and let the subsequent steps take care of themselves.[24] We wait, work, and hope together, a community of pilgrims and exiles on the move toward "the city with foundations, whose architect and builder is God" (Heb. 11:10).

# NOTES

## CHAPTER 1

1. Fact Based Videos, "Interview: Eric Metaxas Interviews Donald Trump with Douglas Mastriano—November 30, 2020," YouTube video, November 30, 2020, https://tinyurl.com/rpbraex2.

2. Emma Green, "A Christian Insurrection," *The Atlantic*, January 8, 2021, https://tinyurl.com/4mfhv8vf.

3. Jack Moline, "Trump Says Biden Will 'Hurt God,' but Such 2020 Posturing Really Hurts Americans," *NBC News*, August 10, 2020, https://tinyurl.com/5fka4wpm.

4. Gustavo Gutiérrez, *A Theology of Liberation*, 15th anniv. ed. (Maryknoll, NY: Orbis, 1988), 36. See Joel Looper, *Bonhoeffer's America: A Land without Reformation* (Waco, TX: Baylor University Press, 2021).

5. "Dramatic Partisan Differences on Blame for January 6 Riots," PRRI, September 15, 2021, https://tinyurl.com/5n7zwra5.

6. Eric Metaxas (@ericmetaxas), "There is no doubt the election was fraudulent," Twitter, January 7, 2021, https://tinyurl.com/2f5chk97.

7. Pastor Gregor Locke (@pastorlocke), "There's a reason one of the most secure buildings on the planet had an easy breach on one of the most important and guarded days in history," Twitter, January 6, 2021, https://tinyurl.com/ye3dk426.

8. Dinesh D'Souza (@DineshDSouza), "This seems consistent with several of the Trumpsters who insist the people who broke the windows were not #MAGA at all," Twitter, January 6, 2021, https://tinyurl.com/bdd7zk3w.

9. Walsh used the full word in his tweet. Matt Walsh (@MattWalshBlog), "An unarmed mother was shot and killed by police in the Capitol today," Twitter, January 7, 2021, https://tinyurl.com/2p8ry6uz.

10. Dr. Darrell Scott (@PastorDScott), "Question: Was today's protest 'mostly peaceful', like all the ones last summer were?," Twitter, January 7, 2021, https://tinyurl.com/bdb7p5r5.

11. Karl Barth, *Die Christliche Gemeinde im Wechsel der Staatsordnungen: Dokumente einer Ungarnreise* (Zürich: Evangelischer Verlag A. G. Zollikon, 1948), 44.

12. Scott Barkley, "Annual Church Profile: Southern Baptist Convention Continues Annual Decline," *The Christian Index*, June 8, 2020, https://tinyurl.com/bdzyx3rt.

13. Ryan Burge, "Why 'Evangelical' Is Becoming Another Word for 'Republican,'" *New York Times,* October 26, 2021, https://tinyurl.com/4b85pb3v.

14. Daniel K. Williams, "White Southern Evangelicals Are Leaving the Church," *Christianity Today*, August 2, 2022, https://tinyurl.com/ya2jvapn.

CHAPTER 2

1. "The Epistle to Diognetus," in *The Apostolic Fathers*, ed. Michael W. Holmes, trans. J. B. Lightfoot and J. R. Harmer (Grand Rapids: Baker, 1999), 541.

2. "The Letters of Ignatius, Bishop of Antioch," in Holmes, *Apostolic Fathers*, 145.

3. Eusebius, *The History of the Church from Christ to Constantine*, ed. Andrew Louth, trans. G. A. Williamson (London: Penguin, 1989), 332–33.

4. Augustine, *City of God against the Pagans*, ed. and trans. R. W. Dyson (Cambridge: Cambridge University Press, 2001), 3.

5. Augustine, *City of God*, 49.

6. Augustine, *City of God*, 235.

7. As quoted in Oliver O'Donovan, *The Desire of the Nations: Rediscovering the Roots of Political Theology* (New York: Cambridge University Press, 1996), 158.

8. Martin Luther, "On Secular Authority," in *Martin Luther: Selections from His Writings*, ed John Dillenberger (New York: Anchor, 1961), 389.

9. John Milton, "The Readie and Easie Way to Establish a Free Commonwealth," *Renascence Editions*, accessed November 26, 2023, https://tinyurl.com/6ka63kaf.

10. Stanley Hauerwas and Ralph Wood, "How the Church Became Invisible: A Christian Reading of the American Literary Tradition," *Religion & Literature* 38, no. 1 (Spring 2006): 61–93.

11. Will Herberg, *Protestant, Catholic, Jew: An Essay in American Religious Sociology* (New York: Anchor, 1960), 23.

12. Herberg, *Protestant, Catholic, Jew*, 13.

13. Noah Lanard, "The Dangerous History behind Netanyahu's

Amalek Rhetoric," *Mother Jones*, November 3, 2023, http://tinyurl.com/2zx26f5b.

14. John Corrigan, "New Israel, New Amalek," in *From Jeremiad to Jihad: Religion, Violence, and America*, ed. John D. Carlson and Jonathan H. Ebel (Berkeley: University of California Press, 2012), 111–16.

15. For more on colonial attitudes toward native Americans and their land, see Jill Lepore, *In the Name of War: King Phillip's War and the Origins of American Identity* (New York: Vintage, 1999).

16. Robert Bellah, "Civil Religion in America," in *Beyond Belief: Essays on Religion in a Post-Traditionalist World* (Berkeley: University of California Press, 1991), 168.

17. Bellah, "Civil Religion in America," 175.

18. Bellah, "Civil Religion in America," 186.

CHAPTER 3

1. Ralph Frammolino, "Graham Says Media Magnified Nixon's Failings and Defeats," *Los Angeles Times*, July 19, 1990, https://tinyurl.com/uyhn7b98.

2. Grant Wacker, *One Soul at a Time: The Story of Billy Graham* (Grand Rapids: Eerdmans, 2019), 178.

3. Aaron Renn, "The Three Worlds of Evangelicalism," *First Things*, February 2022, https://tinyurl.com/3cawhyj2.

4. I doubt it's coincidental that 1994 was the year the Clinton Administration enacted the "don't ask, don't tell" policy regarding gay and lesbian members of the military.

5. Rod Dreher, *The Benedict Option* (New York: Sentinel, 2017), 236.

6. Dreher, *Benedict Option*, 84.

7. Dreher, *Benedict Option*, 88.

8. Countless examples from Dreher's writings could make my point, but just one will do. Dreher moved to Hungary in 2022 because of his reverence for Hungarian President Viktor Orbán and the importance of Christianity to Hungarian culture. In a picture-accompanied tweet from last year, Dreher wrote, "Still can't get over how the Hungarians ended their annual national holiday celebrating the Feast of St Stephen, Hungary's first Christian monarch, with drones making cross above Parliament. You'd never see that over US Capitol on July 4. I know why, but still. Go Hungary!" Rod Dreher (@roddreher), "Still can't get over," X (formerly Twitter), August 23, 2023, https://tinyurl.com/45subajp.

9. PlanoProf, "Jerry Falwell 2 of 3," YouTube video, April 16, 2014, 3:53–4:00, https://tinyurl.com/4cuwyeek.

10. "More than Four-in-Ten U.S. Adults Say the Country Should Be a 'Christian Nation,' but Far Fewer Want Churches to Endorse Candidates, Speak Out on Politics," Pew Research Center, October 24, 2022, https://tinyurl.com/yc6c853m/.

11. "Pastor Robert Jeffress Explains His Support for Trump," *All Things Considered*, NPR, October 16, 2016, https://tinyurl.com/2n6tcr3n.

12. See, for example, Stephanie McCrummen, "The Woman Who Bought a Mountain for God," *The Atlantic*, June 20, 2023, https://tinyurl.com/4hnr4j82.

13. Stephen Wolfe, *The Case for Christian Nationalism* (Moscow, ID: Canon Press, 2022), 11.

14. See, for example, Azar Gat, *Nations: The Long History and Deep Roots of Political Ethnicity and Nationalism* (New York: Cambridge University Press, 2013). The discussion created by Benedict Anderson's extraordinary book *Imagined Communities:*

*Reflections on the Origin and Spread of Nationalism* (New York: Verso, 2016) has at times obscured this reality.

15. Wolfe, *Christian Nationalism*, 145. But for a deceptive and particularly disgusting example of the use to which Wolfe puts this truth, see 169.

16. To cite just one major example, Robert Putnam, "E Pluribus Unum: Diversity and Community in the Twenty-First Century," *Scandinavian Political Studies* 30, no. 2 (2007): 137–74.

17. Wolfe, *Christian Nationalism*, 41.

18. Wolfe, *Christian Nationalism*, 199.

19. I speak against much of the Reformational traditional here and with most Anabaptists. See John Calvin, *Institutes* 4.1.3.

20. Dutch Sheets, "The Re circuiting Continues | Give Him 15 Daily Prayer with Dutch," YouTube, August 9, 2022, https://tinyurl.com/28snjzyd.

21. Molly Worthen, "The Controversialist," *Christianity Today*, April 17, 2009, https://tinyurl.com/3sbu7veb.

22. Karl Barth, *The Epistle to the Romans*, trans. Edwyn Hoskyns, 6th ed. (London: Oxford University Press, 1968), 479.

23. The City Club of Cleveland, "The Reverend Dr. Jerry Falwell 3.26.1982," YouTube video, March 26, 1982, 10:20–11:56, https://tinyurl.com/2p8kx9cv.

24. DEI is a popular acronym for programs in government, businesses, and education that teach and advocate policies that promote diversity, equity, and inclusion.

CHAPTER 4

1. Dmitry Adamsky, *Russian Nuclear Orthodoxy: Religion, Politics, and Strategy* (Stanford: Stanford University Press, 2018), 96.

2. Adamsky, *Russian Nuclear Orthodoxy*, 97.

3. For the massive change in stance toward the West that took place after Putin's reascent to the presidency, see Michael McFaul, *From Cold War to Hot Peace: An American Ambassador in Putin's Russia* (New York: Mariner, 2018).

4. Vladimir Ruvinsky, "Russians Are Not Waiting for a Church Boom," *Moscow Times*, May 29, 2019, https://tinyurl.com/34x84m8m.

5. "Russians Return to Religion, but Not to Church," Pew Research Center, February 10, 2014, https://tinyurl.com/57nudkpe.

6. Vladimir Putin, "On the Historical Unity of Russians and Ukrainians," President of Russia, July 12, 2021, https://tinyurl.com/yzjyey88.

7. See especially Dominic Lieven, *The End of Tsarist Russia: The March to World War I and Revolution* (New York: Penguin, 2015), 51–59.

8. For a thorough treatment of Russia history that addresses many inaccuracies that Putin and other Russian nationalists employ, see Timothy Snyder, *The Making of Modern Ukraine*, fall 2022, Yale University, Podcast, https://tinyurl.com/mv5zbxn6.

9. Here I refer to the old Soviet joke often told by the British political scientist Mark Galeotti: "Russia is a country with a certain future; it is only its past that is unpredictable." Mark Galeotti, *A Short History of Russia: How the World's Largest Country Invented Itself, from Pagans to Putin* (New York: Hanover Square, 2020), epigraph.

10. Adamsky, *Russian Nuclear Orthodoxy*, 20.

11. Adamsky, *Russian Nuclear Orthodoxy*, 186.

12. Lieven, *End of Tsarist Russia*, 367.

13. In Adamsky, *Russian Nuclear Orthodoxy*, 87–88.

14. Adamsky, *Russian Nuclear Orthodoxy*, 30-31, 197-200.

15. Matt Stieb, "Putin Decries U.S. 'Satanism' in Bizarre Speech Annexing Parts of Ukraine," *New York Magazine*, September 30, 2022, https://tinyurl.com/53zjz5yf. See also The Telegraph, "In Full: Vladimir Putin Officially Annexing Four Ukrainian Regions at Moscow Ceremony," YouTube video, September 30, 2022, https://tinyurl.com/4rx5x85v.

16. Julia Davis (@JuliaDavisNews), "Meanwhile in Russia" Twitter, October 25, 2022, https://tinyurl.com/h2msf2vh. See TASS, "В аппарате Совбеза РФ считают все более насущным проведение 'десатанизации' Украины," ТАСС, October 22, 2022, https://tinyurl.com/yc7s24rx.

17. Reporting by Reuters, "Medvedev Says Russia Is Fighting a Sacred Battle against Satan," November 4, 2022, Reuters, https://tinyurl.com/5n6fdb8d.

18. Anna Shamanska, "How Russian State TV Linked Satanists to Ukraine's Leadership," Radio Free Europe, Radio Liberty, August 19, 2014, https://tinyurl.com/24tffbfw.

19. Julia Davis (@JuliaDavisNews), "Meanwhile on Russian State TV: Apti Alaudinov," Twitter, July 17, 2022, https://tinyurl.com/muvut9me.

20. Jonathan Luxmoore, "Dissent from War Is Treason, Said Patriarch Kirill," *Church Times*, April 28, 2023, https://tinyurl.com/2tse5jwu.

21. Russia Desk, "'Other Times Will Come': Patriarch Kirill Deprives Andrey Kuraev of His Holy Dignity," *Eastern Herald*, April 28, 2023, https://tinyurl.com/3jf6xe9h; and Murtaza Hussain, "The Grisly Cult of the Wagner Group's Sledgehammer," *The Intercept*, February 2, 2023, https://tinyurl.com/59m5fkwf.

**CHAPTER 5**

1. Herbert McCabe, *God Matters* (London: Continuum, 2010), 23.

2. Dietrich Bonhoeffer, *Berlin*, Dietrich Bonhoeffer Works 12, ed. Larry Rasmussen, trans. Isabel Best and David Higgins (Minneapolis: Fortress, 2009), 365-73.

**CHAPTER 6**

1. Donald J. Trump (@RealDonaldTrump), "donaldjtrump. com," Truth Social, July 2, 2023, https://tinyurl.com/27ej73k6.

2. Bellah, "Civil Religion in America," 175.

3. Emmanuel Hapsis, "What We Can Learn about Trump from His Favorite President, Andrew Jackson," *KQED*, April 26, 2017, https://tinyurl.com/5n7rw5ax; and David Gessner, "Trump Venerates Teddy Roosevelt, but Roosevelt Would Have Hated Trump," *Washington Post*, September 29, 2020, https://tinyurl. com/4nvf3ppw.

4. Donald J. Trump (@RealDonaldTrump), "I AM NOW GO-ING TO WASHINGTON," Truth Social, August 3, 2023, https:// tinyurl.com/2s498drt.

5. Forbes Breaking News, "Trump Tells Supporters 'I Am the Only One Who Can Save This Nation' after Arraignment," You-Tube video, June 14, 2023, https://tinyurl.com/3mjra4ys.

6. Bess Levin, "Report: Donald Trump, No Joke, Believes What He's Going Through Is like the Crucifixion of Jesus Christ," *Vanity Fair*, April 3, 2023, https://tinyurl.com/5c7tmjsr.

7. Jenna Ellis (@JennaEllisEsq), "But I say unto you," X (formerly Twitter), August 23, 2023, https://tinyurl.com/43va3kh9.

8. Jenna Ellis (@JennaEllisEsq), "This race is far from

over," X (formerly Twitter), September 4, 2023, https://tinyurl.com/w3yda2fv.

9. Donald Trump, interview by Tucker Carlson, posted on Tucker Carlson (@TuckerCarlson), "Ep. 19 Debate Night with Donald J Trump," X (formerly Twitter), August 23, 2023, https://tinyurl.com/nhjkbhka. See 44:55–46:12 for the quotation above.

10. Michael Brown, "What You Don't Know about Donald Trump and the King Cyrus Prophecy," *Townhall*, September 7, 2020, https://tinyurl.com/2b32vmw6; Katherine Stewart, "Why Trump Reigns as King Cyrus," *New York Times*, December 31, 2018, https://tinyurl.com/yuxyv77e; Daniel Block, "Is Trump Our Cyrus? The Old Testament Case for Yes and No," *Christianity Today*, October 29, 2018, https://tinyurl.com/2f7xv2t6.

11. Chris Cilliza, "Yes, Donald Trump Really Believes He's 'the Chosen One,'" *CNN*, August 24, 2019, https://tinyurl.com/5e3d8jck.

12. Susan B. Glasser, "'I Am the Only One': Trump's Messianic 2024 Message," *New Yorker*, June 15, 2023, https://tinyurl.com/4erj2f9w.

13. Note actor Jim Caviezel's sense that Trump is a "new Moses." Ed Kilgore, "New Moses Is a New Sign of Christian Right's Trump Confusion. Trump Used to Be Their Unwitting Agent of God. Now He's a Religious Leader?," *New Yorker*, July 23, 2023, https://tinyurl.com/44rjv25c.

14. Russell Moore, "Trumpism Has Changed Evangelicalism, Not the Other Way Around, Says Author," interview by *Morning Joe*, MSNBC, July 25, 2023, https://tinyurl.com/444pkb46.

15. Patriot Takes (@patriottakes), "Michael Flynn warns dark forces," Twitter, August 10, 2023, https://tinyurl.com/545bbbv4.

16. Patriot Takes (@patriottakes), "In a Christian Nationalist rant, Michael Flynn told pastors," Twitter, August 9, 2023, https://tinyurl.com/ys2zzr5n.

17. Barna Group, "One in Three Practicing Christians Has Stopped Attending Church during the Pandemic," *Barna*, July 8, 2020, https://tinyurl.com/68sufm38.

18. Wendy Wang, "The Decline in Church Attendance in COVID America," Institute for Family Studies, January 20, 2022, https://tinyurl.com/mryfkj6k.

19. See the graph provided here, the data for which came from the 2020 Faith Communities Today survey. "Study: Attendance at US Religious Congregations Halved Since 2000," *Banner*, October 22, 2021, https://tinyurl.com/3pt4r4tp.

20. Political scientist Ryan Burge drew this data from the Cooperative Election Survey. (@ryanburge), "The only group that has really seen a drop," Twitter, February 12, 2023, https://tinyurl.com/y5aphmnn.

21. E.g., Jake Meador, "The Misunderstood Reason Millions of Americans Stopped Going to Church," *The Atlantic*, July 29, 2023, https://tinyurl.com/4xnc346c; and Brandon Flannery, "I Asked People Why They're Leaving Christianity, and Here's What I Heard," *Baptist News*, December 13, 2022, https://tinyurl.com/mtfdwcs2.

22. Williams, "White Southern Evangelicals."

23. Harald Jähner, *Aftermath: Life in the Fallout of the Third Reich, 1945–1955*, trans. Shaun Whiteside (New York: Knopf, 2022), 15.

24. Dietrich Bonhoeffer, *Ethics*, Dietrich Bonhoeffer Works 6 (Minneapolis: Fortress, 2005), 224–25.

# BIBLIOGRAPHY

Adamsky, Dmitry. *Russian Nuclear Orthodoxy: Religion, Politics, and Strategy.* Stanford: Stanford University Press, 2018.

Anderson, Benedict. *Imagined Communities: Reflections on the Origin and Spread of Nationalism.* New York: Verso, 2016.

Augustine. *City of God against the Pagans.* Edited and translated by R. W. Dyson. Cambridge: Cambridge University Press, 2001.

Barkley, Scott. "Annual Church Profile: Southern Baptist Convention Continues Annual Decline." *Christian Index.* June 8, 2020. https://tinyurl.com/bdzyx3rt.

The Barna Group. "One in Three Practicing Christians Has Stopped Attending Church during the Pandemic." *Barna.* July 8, 2020. https://tinyurl.com/68sufm38.

Barth, Karl. *Die Christliche Gemeinde im Wechsel der Staatsordnungen: Dokumente einer Ungarnreise.* Zürich: Evangelischer Verlag A. G. Zollikon, 1948.

———. *The Epistle to the Romans.* Translated by Edwyn Hoskyns. 6th ed. London: Oxford University Press, 1968.

Bellah, Robert. "Civil Religion in America." In *Beyond Belief: Essays on Religion in a Post-Traditionalist World*, 168–89. Berkeley: University of California Press, 1991.

Block, Daniel. "Is Trump Our Cyrus? The Old Testament Case for Yes and No." *Christianity Today*, October 29, 2018. https://tinyurl.com/2f7xv2t6.

Bonhoeffer, Dietrich. *Berlin*. Dietrich Bonhoeffer Works 12. Edited by Larry Rasmussen. Translated by Isabel Best and David Higgins. Minneapolis: Fortress, 2009.

———. *Ethics*. Dietrich Bonhoeffer Works 6. Edited by Clifford Green. Translated by Reinhard Krauss, Charles C. West, and Douglas W. Stott. Minneapolis: Fortress, 2006.

Brown, Michael. "What You Don't Know about Donald Trump and the King Cyrus Prophecy." *Townhall*, September 7, 2020. https://tinyurl.com/2b32vmw6.

Burge, Ryan. "Why 'Evangelical' Is Becoming Another Word for 'Republican.'" *New York Times*, October 26, 2021. https://tinyurl.com/4b85pb3v.

Cilliza, Chris. "Yes, Donald Trump Really Believes He's 'the Chosen One.'" *CNN*. August 24, 2019. https://tinyurl.com/5e3d8jck.

The City Club of Cleveland. "The Reverend Dr. Jerry Falwell 3.26.1982." YouTube video. March 26, 1982. https://tinyurl.com/2p8kx9cv.

Corrigan, John. "New Israel, New Amalek." In *From Jeremiad to Jihad: Religion, Violence, and America*, edited by John D. Carlson and Jonathan H. Ebel, 111–27. Berkeley: University of California Press, 2012.

"Dramatic Partisan Differences on Blame for January 6 Riots." PRRI. September 15, 2021. https://tinyurl.com/5n7zwra5.

Dreher, Rod. *The Benedict Option: A Strategy for Christians in a Post-Christian Nation.* New York: Sentinel, 2017.

"The Epistle to Diognetus." In *The Apostolic Fathers*, edited by Michael W. Holmes, translated by J. B. Lightfoot and J. R. Harmer. Grand Rapids: Baker, 1992.

Eusebius. *The History of the Church from Christ to Constantine.* Edited by Andrew Louth. Translated by G. A. Williamson. London: Penguin, 1989.

Fact Based Videos. "Interview: Eric Metaxas Interviews Donald Trump with Douglas Mastriano—November 30, 2020." YouTube video. November 30, 2020. https://tinyurl.com/rpbraex2.

Flannery, Brandon. "I Asked People Why They're Leaving Christianity, and Here's What I Heard." *Baptist News.* December 13, 2022. https://tinyurl.com/mtfdwcs2.

Forbes Breaking News. "Trump Tells Supporters 'I Am the Only One Who Can Save This Nation' After Arraignment." YouTube video. June 14, 2023. https://tinyurl.com/3mjra4ys.

Frammolino, Ralph. "Graham Says Media Magnified Nixon's Failings and Defeats." *Los Angeles Times*, July 19, 1990. https://tinyurl.com/uyhn7b98.

Galeotti, Mark. *A Short History of Russia: How the World's Largest Country Invented Itself, from Pagans to Putin.* New York: Hanover Square, 2020.

Gat, Azar. *Nations: The Long History and Deep Roots of Political Ethnicity and Nationalism.* New York: Cambridge University Press, 2013.

Gessner, David. "Trump Venerates Teddy Roosevelt, but Roosevelt Would Have Hated Trump." *Washington Post*, September 29, 2020. https://tinyurl.com/4nvf3ppw.

Glasser, Susan B. "'I Am the Only One': Trump's Messianic 2024 Message." *New Yorker*, June 15, 2023. https://tinyurl.com/4erj2f9w.

Green, Emma. "A Christian Insurrection." *The Atlantic*, January 8, 2021. https://tinyurl.com/4mfhv8vf.

Gutiérrez, Gustavo. *A Theology of Liberation*. 15th anniv. ed. Maryknoll, NY: Orbis, 1988.

Hapsis, Emmanuel. "What We Can Learn about Trump from His Favorite President, Andrew Jackson." *KQED*. April 26, 2017. https://tinyurl.com/5n7rw5ax.

Hauerwas, Stanley, and Ralph Wood. "How the Church Became Invisible: A Christian Reading of the American Literary Tradition." *Religion & Literature* 38, no. 1 (Spring 2006): 61–93.

Herberg, Will. *Protestant, Catholic, Jew: An Essay in American Religious Sociology*. New York: Anchor, 1960.

Holmes, Michael W., ed. *The Apostolic Fathers*. Translated by J. B. Lightfoot and J. R. Harmer. Grand Rapids: Baker, 1992.

Hussain, Murtaza. "The Grisly Cult of the Wagner Group's Sledgehammer." *The Intercept*. February 2, 2023. https://tinyurl.com/59m5fkwf.

Ignatius of Antioch. "The Letters to Ignatius, Bishop of Antioch." In *The Apostolic Fathers*, edited by Michael W. Holmes, translated by J. B. Lightfoot and J. R. Harmer. Grand Rapids: Baker, 1992.

Jähner, Harald. *Aftermath: Life in the Fallout of the Third Reich, 1945–1955*. Translated by Shaun Whiteside. New York: Knopf, 2022.

Kilgore, Ed. "New Moses Is a New Sign of Christian Right's Trump Confusion. Trump Used to Be Their Unwitting

Agent of God. Now He's a Religious Leader?" *New Yorker*, July 23, 2023. https://tinyurl.com/44rjv25c.

Lepore, Jill. *In the Name of War: King Phillip's War and the Origins of American Identity*. New York: Vintage, 1999.

Levin, Bess. "Report: Donald Trump, No Joke, Believes What He's Going Through Is like the Crucifixion of Jesus Christ." *Vanity Fair*, April 3, 2023. https://tinyurl.com/5c7tmjsr.

Lieven, Dominic. *The End of Tsarist Russia: The March to World War I and Revolution*. New York: Penguin, 2015.

Looper, Joel. *Bonhoeffer's America: A Land without Reformation*. Waco, TX: Baylor University Press, 2021.

Luther, Martin. "On Secular Authority." In *Martin Luther: Selections from His Writings*, edited by John Dillenberger. New York: Anchor, 1961.

Luxmoore, Jonathan. "Dissent from War Is Treason, Said Patriarch Kirill." *Church Times*, April 28, 2023. https://tinyurl.com/2tse5jwu.

McCabe, Herbert. *God Matters*. London: Continuum, 2010.

McCrummen, Stephanie. "The Woman Who Bought a Mountain for God." *The Atlantic*, June 20, 2023. https://tinyurl.com/4hnr4j82.

McFaul, Michael. *From Cold War to Hot Peace: An American Ambassador in Putin's Russia*. New York: Mariner, 2018.

Meador, Jake. "The Misunderstood Reason Millions of Americans Stopped Going to Church." *The Atlantic*, July 29, 2023. https://tinyurl.com/4xnc346c.

"Medvedev Says Russia Is Fighting a Sacred Battle against Satan." *Reuters*, November 4, 2022. https://tinyurl.com/5n6fdb8d.

Moline, Jack. "Trump Says Biden Will 'Hurt God,' but Such

2020 Posturing Really Hurts Americans." *NBC News*. August 10, 2020. https://tinyurl.com/5fka4wpm.

Moore, Russell. "Trumpism Has Changed Evangelicalism, Not the Other Way Around, Says Author." Interview by *Morning Joe*. MSNBC. July 25, 2023. https://tinyurl.com/444pkb46.

"More than Four-in-Ten U.S. Adults Say the Country Should Be a 'Christian Nation,' but Far Fewer Want Churches to Endorse Candidates, Speak Out on Politics." Pew Research Center. October 24, 2022. https://tinyurl.com/yc6c853m.

O'Donovan, Oliver. *The Desire of the Nations: Rediscovering the Roots of Political Theology*. New York: Cambridge University Press, 1996.

PlanoProf. "Jerry Falwell 2 of 3." YouTube video. April 16, 2014. 3:53–4:00. https://tinyurl.com/4cuwyeek.

Putin, Vladimir. "On the Historical Unity of Russians and Ukrainians." President of Russia. July 12, 2021. https://tinyurl.com/yzjyey88.

Putnam, Robert. "E Pluribus Unum: Diversity and Community in the Twenty-first Century." *Scandinavian Political Studies* 30, no. 2 (2007): 137–74.

Renn, Aaron. "The Three Worlds of Evangelicalism." *First Things*, February 2022. https://tinyurl.com/3cawhyj2.

Russia Desk. "'Other Times Will Come': Patriarch Kirill Deprives Andrey Kuraev of His Holy Dignity." *Eastern Herald*, April 28, 2023. https://tinyurl.com/3jf6xe9h.

"Russians Return to Religion, but Not to Church." Pew Research Center. February 10, 2014. https://tinyurl.com/57nudkpe.

Ruvinsky, Vladimir. "Russians Are Not Waiting for a Church

Boom." *Moscow Times,* May 29, 2019. https://tinyurl. com/34x84m8m.

Shamanska, Anna. "How Russian State TV Linked Satanists to Ukraine's Leadership." *Radio Free Europe, Radio Liberty.* August 19, 2014. https://tinyurl.com/24tffbfw.

Sheets, Dutch. "The Re circuiting Continues | Give Him 15 Daily Prayer with Dutch." YouTube video. August 9, 2022. https://tinyurl.com/28snjzyd.

Smietana, Bob. "Study: Attendance at US Religious Congregations Halved since 2000." *Banner,* October 22, 2021. https://tinyurl.com/3pt4r4tp.

Snyder, Timothy. *The Making of Modern Ukraine.* Podcast. Yale University. Fall 2022. https://tinyurl.com/mv5zbxn6.

Stewart, Katherine. "Why Trump Reigns as King Cyrus." *New York Times,* December 31, 2018. https://tinyurl.com/53zjz5yf.

Stieb, Matt. "Putin Decries U.S. 'Satanism' in Bizarre Speech Annexing Parts of Ukraine." *New York Magazine,* September 30, 2022. https://tinyurl.com/53zjz5yf.

TASS. "В аппарате Совбеза РФ считают все более насущным проведение 'десатанизации' Украины." ТАСС. October 22, 2022. https://tinyurl.com/yc7s24rx.

The Telegraph. "In Full: Vladimir Putin Officially Annexing Four Ukrainian Regions at Moscow Ceremony." YouTube video. September 30, 2022. https://tinyurl.com/4rx5x85v.

Wacker, Grant. *One Soul at a Time: The Story of Billy Graham.* Grand Rapids: Eerdmans, 2019.

Wang, Wendy. "The Decline in Church Attendance in COVID America." Institute for Family Studies. January 20, 2022. https://tinyurl.com/mryfkj6k.

Williams, Daniel K. "White Southern Evangelicals Are Leaving the Church." *Christianity Today*, August 2, 2022. https://tinyurl.com/ya2jvapn.

Wolfe, Stephen. *The Case for Christian Nationalism*. Moscow, ID: Canon Press, 2022.

Worthen, Molly. "The Controversialist." *Christianity Today*, April 17, 2009. https://tinyurl.com/3sbu7veb.

# SUBJECT INDEX

# SCRIPTURE INDEX